GETTING
YOURSELF
SPONSORED

GETTING YOURSELF SPONSORED

For AUTHORS, ASSOCIATIONS,
or ANY BUSINESS...
YOUR BLUEPRINT *to* UNLOCK BRAND
NEW REVENUE STREAMS

Ron Seaver

Published by Advantage, Charleston, South Carolina.
Member of Advantage Media Group.

ADVANTAGE is a registered trademark and the Advantage colophon is a trademark of Advantage Media Group, Inc.

Printed in the United States of America.

ISBN: 978-1-59932-278-0
LCCN: 2011912568

This publication is designed to provide accurate and authoritative information in regard to the subject matter covered. It is sold with the understanding that the publisher is not engaged in rendering legal, accounting, or other professional services. If legal advice or other expert assistance is required, the services of a competent professional person should be sought.

Advantage Media Group is proud to be a part of the Tree Neutral® program. Tree Neutral offsets the number of trees consumed in the production and printing of this book by taking proactive steps such as planting trees in direct proportion to the number of trees used to print books. To learn more about Tree Neutral, please visit www.treeneutral.com. To learn more about Advantage's commitment to being a responsible steward of the environment, please visit www.advantagefamily.com/green

Advantage Media Group is a leading publisher of business, motivation, and self-help authors. Do you have a manuscript or book idea that you would like to have considered for publication? Please visit www.amgbook.com or call 1.866.775.1696

To Christy -
For all your love, belief and support.

Contents

Chapter One

"Deal Me In!"

"Pass the Salt?"

The conversation started innocently enough. Ten strangers put together at one table during a lunch break at a conference, and between the salad course and the chicken entrée, someone got it started by turning to the person next to him and asking:

"So, what do YOU do?"

And so it began. Around the table with each of us introducing ourselves and explaining what we did for a living. That's not unusual—happens almost every conference going on out there. But what made this one so special was that it was a "conference on conferences." In other words, this was a meeting for people who either already put on meetings, or for those who were seriously thinking about doing just that.

Little did I realize when the question started making its way around the table that afternoon that the result would wind up with me writing this book.

For when it finally landed on me, I answered it… and then sent it back around the table—with a thought-provoking change.

"Let's go around one more time, only this time, tell me who your sponsors are…"

The silence was deafening.

The others at the table looked mystified. "Sponsors? OUR sponsors? I…I… well, um— we don't really HAVE any sponsors."

Every single member at that table—in fact, everyone I asked throughout that three-day conference—either had never thought about getting sponsors for their meeting, conferences or association gatherings. Or maybe they had thought about it but truly had no clue as to how to go about landing a sponsor.

Here are three main questions that materialized:

- How does someone go about getting someone to sponsor his or her property?

- When you do get a potential sponsor interested, how much should you consider charging them?

- What should you give them in return?

I'm going to answer these questions, and a whole lot of other ones, in the pages that follow. Because if you're in the business of putting on group gatherings, or you've got a viable newsletter or e-zine, you really owe it to your bottom line to allow outsiders to give you their money. It's good for them, it's good for your clients and customers, and best of all, it's good for *you!*

Who IS This Guy Anyway?

So, let's circle up the chairs right here because class is about to start. As we do, I will start by telling you a little bit about myself.

Aside from the fact that I'm a native of New Hampshire, and am a "born 'n bred" Red Sox fan, I certainly didn't start out with a plan to spend my life in the world of sponsorship. Instead, I looked to spend my life in the advertising industry. After I received my degree from the Newhouse School at Syracuse University in upstate New York, I then set about the task of trying to find a job in the advertising industry.

The only problem was—I found out that I hated advertising! Well, maybe hate's too strong a word. I loved the creative process but I didn't much cotton to all the politics that went with it.

So I tried my hand at a number of different things, from bartending to hotel work and all points in between. (A total of eight jobs in my first five years out of school, which has got to be some kind of record.)

By the ripe old age of 26, all I'd managed to compile was a good-sized list of all the things I *didn't* want to do with the rest of my life, and no clue as to what in the world I wanted to do for a living. That's when it dawned on me. If all else fails, why not go with my passion?

And for me, my passion has always been baseball. I loved playing it, and I loved watching it. I had just moved to San Diego so why not reach out to the local team and see if I could convince the San Diego Padres that I was the only thing keeping them from a winning team?

Initially I spent a year trying to sell folks tickets over the phone. (Yes, I was the guy calling you up at dinner time. Sorry about that!)

As much as I loved working for a major league baseball team, it really all came together for me in January 1984 when I got the chance to go to work in the club's Promotions Department. Now that was fun!

By the end of the year I was not only moving boxes and writing scoreboard announcements, I was also trying my hand at something I would really come to love — selling sponsorships.

I had the good fortune to go to work for Andy Strasberg, a man who would not only become my mentor, but also one of my very best friends. He patiently taught me everything he knew about the business of selling and servicing sponsorships. I can honestly tell you that I'd still be out there stumbling around aimlessly had I not had the good fortune to have him take me under his wing.

During my time with the Padres, I ultimately grew the team's sponsorships from a roster of ten to a total of 36 and sold and serviced everyone from Budweiser to Chevrolet...Bank of America to Coca-Cola. Working with all these dynamic and diverse companies really gave me a broad understanding of all of the dynamics that make up an effective sponsorship.

On the eve of 1991, after eight years with the Padres, I went over to the other side of the table and became vice president for what was then the largest West Coast-based sports marketing agency, where I bought and serviced local, regional and national campaigns for such companies as Ralston-Purina, Gillette USA, Denny's Restaurants, Orville Reddenbacher Popcorn, Upper Deck Trading Cards, Evian Waters of France and Royal Oak Charcoal. From the Olympics, to NFL football and professional golf, I was responsible for creating programs and promotions that would help clients sell more of their products. That too proved to be great fun. And along the way, I acquired a different perspective of the sponsorship equation—the sponsor's view of sponsorship.

And finally, in 1994 I left that agency to start one of my own, Seaver Marketing Group, which is where I am to this day. Starting my own agency gave me the chance to chase a dream and to work on an idea I'd first had back in my Major League Baseball days in the late 1980s. Beginning that year, the fall of 1994, we started working on launching our own event, The National Sports Forum (Sports Forum). It was created as an event that would annually bring together the top marketing, ticket sales, sponsorship, and advertising executives from the NFL, MLB, NBA, NHL, Major League Soccer, auto racing and horse racing. In short, it's become about as close to a United Nations type gathering of team and event sports as you're going to find under one roof.

Not that it was an overnight success—it definitely wasn't. In fact, our first efforts to launch the Sports Forum were nothing short of a disaster. With ten speakers but only three folks registered, we had no choice but to cancel three weeks out. (At a cost of $65,000... ouch!)

But we refused to give it up. My thought was, if we could only get it going and then hang in there long enough to have people start trying it, it would work. And to help us with that, we thought it might also prove beneficial to build a steering committee of team and agency leaders who would guide our process. It definitely wasn't easy, but it worked! We actually got the first-ever Sports Forum launched in January 1996. It was small, with an audience of 35 attendees that year, but it was a start! All told, we were now two years working on it, and we were down over $100,000. But, fortunately, with a supportive wife and the hard efforts of a number of great people over the years, we kept at it. And it's kept growing. Now, 17 years later, that first year's initial 35 attendees has now grown to about 750 executives. And along the way, we've added a sold-out trade show each January—plus an entire host of sponsors.

Which brings us back almost full circle.

Through it all there's been one consistency that's been woven through these past 28 years. And that's been an active background in creating, selling and servicing sponsorships. All told, I've had a hand in putting together well over 1,500 sponsorship packages over the years, ranging in size from $1,500 packages to those close to $1 million each—with stops at all points in between.

Not that any of this will show up on the final exam, but I think it's important as we get started here that you know I've had a lot of background doing this. As they say, "talk the talk if you've walked the walk."

So let's get started, shall we?

Chapter Two

"What've we GOT Here, Anyway?"

Welcome to the Wild, Wild World of Sponsorship!

I f you're thinking about getting serious about this—then you should begin by learning as much as you can about sponsorships and that starts with a solid definition of what sponsorships are…

The Best Definition of Sponsorship I've Ever Seen

There's an organization in Chicago named IEG, Inc., which has been around since the mid-80's. For my money, they're the foremost experts on all things sponsorship related and, with grateful recognition and appreciation, let me start by giving you IEG's definition for the word "sponsorship:"

Spon*sor*ship (noun): *"The trading of cash and/or in-kind products or services in exchange for the right to be officially affiliated with your team, event or program."*

NOTE: As you start broadening your education about sponsorship, I highly recommend becoming familiar with IEG. The company puts out an excellent newsletter that tracks and reports on all things sponsorship-related. Visit them on the web at www.sponsorship.com.

What Do Sponsors Sponsor?

So, what gets sponsored? Well, for one, there are sporting events. That one you probably knew about. Sports are really where the whole industry of sponsorship got started. You can go back to the early days of professional sports here in America and you'll find that it was early on that ball clubs learned the value of target market promotions. There were value-added events and products that got people off of their couches and into the ballparks. "Ladies Day," "Bat Day" and "Cap Night" are just some of the early promotions ball clubs are still using effectively today.

That went on for years until sometime around the early 1970's, when I'm told clubs started adding the icing to the cake. That's when someone figured out they could get area businesses to pay an advertising fee in exchange for attaching their name to the promotion as the provider of that game's special activity, event or premium. It was then that sponsorship was born.

In the early days, sports were about the only thing that got sponsored. Even as late as the mid-80's, sports accounted for about 96% of all the sponsorship dollars being spent out in the market, says IEG. But something was beginning to change.

Little by little, other events started recognizing the growing number of dollars that were annually pouring into the sports industry and started thinking, "If it can work for them, why can't it work for us?"

And the truth is, it does! Today, sports teams and sporting events have seen their virtual monopoly on sponsorship start to erode as corporate America branches out into underwriting such things as fairs, festivals, music concerts, charitable events, museums, theaters and the like. In addition, small business owners—ones just like you—who are putting on boot camps, publishing newsletters and creating info-products, are also vehicles for sponsorships.

True sports still gain the "lion's share" of the sponsorship dollars spent out there, but the gap continues to narrow. Today, according to IEG, the sponsorship pie breaks out as follows:

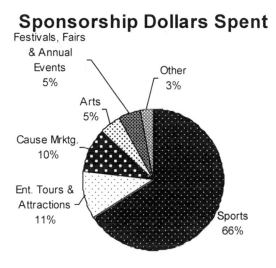

Sponsorship Dollars Spent

Festivals, Fairs & Annual Events 5%

Other 3%

Arts 5%

Cause Mrktg. 10%

Ent. Tours & Attractions 11%

Sports 66%

It's All About the Benjamins – The Dollars Spent Each Year on Sponsorship

Taking that to the next step, the question you're probably asking yourself is "What kind of money is being spent on sponsorships each year?"

Great question! The money, as you're about to see, is nothing short of staggering. And best of all, it just continues to grow larger and larger each year.

Growth of Sponsorship Spend Nationally over the Years

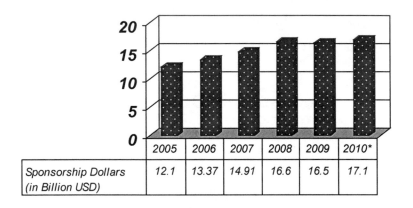

	2005	2006	2007	2008	2009	2010*
Sponsorship Dollars (in Billion USD)	12.1	13.37	14.91	16.6	16.5	17.1

*Projected Sponsorship Spending
(SOURCE: *IEG, Inc. – www.sponsorship.com*)

One of the hottest "newcomers" on the sponsorship arena is the increase in the amount of money spent on underwriting meetings, conferences and associations.

According to Jim Andrews, executive editor of IEG's newsletter, *Special Events Report*:

"This year (2010)... it is projected that corporate spend on sponsoring meetings and associations alone will eclipse **half a billion dollars.**"

That's got to grab your attention—I know it did mine. However, those kinds of dollars have probably got you wondering, "Why would a company want to spend that kind of money on sponsoring a meeting?"

The answer is simple really. And it has its roots in what sponsorship really is: sponsorship is nothing more and nothing less than just another kind of advertising. It's one more way in which a company can use its money to get its name out there in front of its target market.

A Little Role Playing to Help You Understand WHY Sponsors Sponsor

It might be easier to understand all this if we put you through a little exercise. We're going to put you in the role of a typical American business out there trying to compete in an ever-competitive world.

For this role play we're going to transform you into a store manager. Poof! You're now the proud owner of Milty's Office Supply Depot and your livelihood from this point forward depends largely on your ability to get the locals in the community to come through your doors and buy their office staples from you.

What's the first thing you need to do? That's right—get busy and let folks know your doors are open and you're in business! You've got to let people know who you are, what you are, what you've got, when your store is open, and lastly, and most importantly, why they should do business with you!

In short, you've got to advertise.

Why advertise? Well, the best answer to that question is to quote the legendary PT Barnum, one of the world's foremost promoters who put it best when he proclaimed "A funny thing happens when you stop advertising...nothing!"

PT's right. If folks don't know about you, they can't buy from you! Therefore, as the new owner of Milty's Office Supply Depot, you've got your work cut out for you. You've got to let people know you're in business.

But how to do it?

Well, there's **television advertising,** of course. Heaven knows there's a huge audience out there in TV land. But, as effective as television is, it's terribly expensive. Buying 30-seconds' worth of TV time, even just in your local market, can cost you literally thousands of dollars. (That's a lot of pencil erasers and notepads!) On top of this per spot cost, know that you can't just buy one spot and hope to break through to your target market. Nope—you've got to buy lots of spots. If you hope to break through to your crowd and be heard, you've got to buy a lot of repetition. (And, trust me, that ain't cheap!) Even if money were no object to you, which shows do you buy? There're over 120 channels out there running 24-hours a day. Better choose wisely.

Okay, let's skip TV advertising.

How about **radio?** Not a bad choice, but like television, the radio dial is also crowded. AM or FM? Again, you're going to need to buy a large schedule to hopefully reach your target audience. Radio's not nearly as expensive as television, but you should know radio is what they call an "active medium." With television, people sit around and watch it, but radio is generally something folks listen to when they're engaged in something else. They're driving to work, out jogging, lying out on the beach, talking to friends, so even if you do reach your target market, are they listening to you? Or have they mentally tuned out as they're driving down the highway?

Newspapers? Not horrible, but take a hard look at those circulation numbers before you buy. What you'll discover is that people are increasingly migrating away from the daily newspaper. Who has time to read the paper every day? Not many. And you've got to hope that those who do read the daily will notice your quarter page ad tucked on the corner of page 16 of the front section.

Billboards, bus cards, Internet advertising — it's a mixed bag out there. And all of them with their own pluses and minuses.

The plus is visibility, which is a good thing. But one of the biggest minuses you're faced with is the reality that you're definitely not alone out there. You and 20,000 other brands, companies and services are also trying to get the word out to your target market about their company as well. Each of these folks is trying to accomplish the same thing you are—get the message out and the customers in. And the result is a staggering amount of advertising clutter out there.

With so many companies, brands, products and services all trying to get their names out there, consumers today are literally barraged with commercial messages. So much so that researchers have estimated that every American consumer today is exposed to somewhere between 3,500 and 5,000 commercial 'stimuli' each and every day!

Needless to say, that's a massive amount of advertising. So much so that just about the only thing that keeps our respective heads from exploding is that we've somehow managed to grow an internal ad filter to tune out just about all of it.

In fact, advertising clutter today has gotten so bad that it's spawned its own cottage industry. We can thank advertising clutter for single-handedly putting a Ti-Vo or digital video recorder into just about everyone's living room. And the advent of satellite radio? One of satellite's biggest selling points is that it helps us to by-pass advertising clutter. Even Congress has stepped in with "do not call" and "do not fax" laws. (Is it just me, or does it seem like every time we invent something to help us get our message out there, someone else comes out with something to block it?)

As the store manager for Milty's Office Supply Depot, what are you going to do?

Well, what about sponsorship?

It's a way of getting the word out there about your products and services to your market with the desired result that those people will be impacted enough to want to do business with you.

And, as with other forms of more traditional advertising, sponsorship has its flaws. It too has its "pluses and minuses."

For one thing, with sponsorship, you're not going to be reaching as *many* target consumers as you would with the more mass media forms of advertising. (Not unless the event or product you're having sponsored is large enough to enable you to buy mass media to help you promote your meeting or conference.)

Then again, chances are you're not going to be charging your sponsor the $3 million they're asking for 30 seconds worth of airtime on next year's Super Bowl either! Three million dollars for 30 seconds worth of airtime? I don't know about you, but that sure seems like a mind-boggling sum of money to me. We're talking 30 seconds or about how long it took you to read these last couple of paragraphs. And it cost you $3 million. I sure hope you weren't out using the bathroom when my spot came on!

But you might be reading this thinking, "Hmmmm, I don't know. Sponsorship isn't as 'in their face' with the message as say a TV spot or a direct mail flyer is."

And you'd be right—but think about it. That's actually a good thing, not a bad thing.

Sponsorship is subtle. It flies below the radar screen and as such, it often goes undetected by those personal ad filters I just talked about. Your target market, for the most part, won't filter out the sponsor message because it hits them while they're actively engaged in a desired activity.

Think about the last time you were in a stadium watching a ballgame. You undoubtedly looked up at the scoreboard dozens of times during the contest to see what the score was, the count, how much time was left in the quarter, the yards still needed to get to the next first down and so forth. And every time you looked up on the scoreboard, there it was — the sign right next to the game clock telling you how delicious an ice cold Coca-Cola would be right about now. Time and time again. No doubt three hours (and two Cokes from the concession stand later) you went home from the game with a smile on your face and your wallet a few dollars lighter. That sign sitting there as it did for three hours did its work. And no doubt, that sign was just one piece of Coca-Cola's sponsorship package.

Let's stay in the sports world for another minute. Have you ever gone to the stadium or arena and received a baseball cap or a sports bag as you walked through the turnstile? Maybe you were there when they set off a post-game fireworks show? Or perhaps they were having a game-long salute to the military?

Chances are excellent that the item you received, or spectacle you witnessed that night was brought to you by an outside company. In fact, the on-air announcers talked about this event for weeks leading up to cap night or the majestic Fourth of July Fireworks Show—all made possible by XYZ Company.

That night, as the ushers handed you your baseball cap, there on the side of the cap was stitched the sponsoring company's name. The public address announcer welcomed everyone that night to cap night brought to you by XYZ Company and the president or local general manager of the company came and threw out the ceremonial first pitch or coin flip before he or she retired to the special skybox suite the club had set aside for them. That's sponsorship.

Here's an example of sponsorship at work in the world of theatre and music. Have you ever gone to the opening of a private invitation-only show in which the president of the sponsoring company comes out front before the festivities start to say a few words about that evening's performance and why his or her company is proud to help support it? Most of us have.

What you may not have consciously noticed is that the sponsoring company's name was imprinted boldly on top of all of the tickets that night? Or that the lobby had banners strategically placed welcoming you to the event compliments of XYZ Company—placed so that it was the first thing you saw when you walked into the theater, and the last thing you saw going home?

And let's take a closer look. There's a good chance that the first four center rows were blocked off for special VIP guests. And after the show, while you were in the parking lot fighting the traffic to get out, four or five-dozen special guests headed upstairs at the theater to enjoy a private post-event party with that evening's artist.

These are all examples of sponsorship in action—giving the sponsoring company access and exposure to their target market and compelling people to take some sort of action. Done effectively, sponsorship not only helps to get the word out there, but, along with that word, it helps motivate folks to come do some business with the host company. And believe me when I tell you...it works.

Case in Point – "Denny's Trivia Tuesdays"

Here's an example of all the elements of sponsorship in action:

Several years ago, while working for the San Diego Padres, I was approached by Denny's Restaurants before the season started about coming up with a promotion that would not only promote Denny's, but help drive our fans into any of their San Diego-area restaurants.

I came up with a season-long promotion called "Denny's Restaurants Trivia Tuesdays." All that season, at every Padres' Tuesday home game, we would hand out a special scratch-off game card to each of our fans as they came into the ballpark that night. Each game card had the Padres logo printed right next to that for Denny's Restaurants and each game card contained a baseball trivia question. Below each question were three possible scratch-off answers—only one of which was correct. The fans job then was to answer the question by looking at the three possible answers and scratching off the box next to the answer selected. (Note: All told we'd come up with close to 300 different questions and mixed them up. In that way the likelihood that any two fans walking through the turnstiles next to each other getting the same trivia question were fairly remote.)

The stakes were high. Answer your trivia question correctly and you won a free Denny's "Grand Slam Breakfast." So select wisely.

But here's the best part—even if you got it wrong you were a winner! Answer the question incorrectly, and you were still able to redeem your "Trivia Tuesdays" card at any Denny's Restaurant in San Diego County. Only instead of a Grand Slam Breakfast, wrong answers received a free slice of Denny's delicious pie.

There were no losers! And that was especially true for all the Denny's Restaurants that season in San Diego. For in addition to receiving six months' worth of in-stadium public address announcements and scoreboard messages, not to mention well over a hundred over-the-air TV and radio drop-in messages during our play-by-play broadcasts, Denny's realized an average redemption of over 35% of these cards coming back into their stores after each and every Tuesday home game that season.

Maybe you're reading this thinking, "What's so great about that? Denny's must have hated giving away all that free food!"

I'm sure they weren't overjoyed at the prospect of giving *anything* away; however, they were smart enough to realize that putting the hens on overtime and frying up a couple thousand pieces of ham was a small price to pay for the tremendous onslaught of business pouring through their doors every week.

Think about it, how many of our fans came to their area Denny's Restaurants all alone? Not many. They'd bring someone with them or, better yet, bring three someones with them! And even if they do go by themselves, they're going to want a cup of coffee or a glass of juice to go with their Grand Slam Breakfast, agreed?

And what about those out there who scratched off the wrong box? Thousands of them now made it their business to find the closest Denny's Restaurant to their home or office and got themselves in there for a free slice of pie. We're talking literally thousands and thousands of customers! (And let me ask you—who's going to make that trip to sit there for just a slice of pie? Nobody. They're going to come in, probably with at least one other cash-paying guest, and order up a burger, fries and a soft drink to go with their "free" slice of pie.) Suffice it to say—the return was sensational.

Denny's loved this promotion and their sponsorship of the Padres. So much so that at the end of the year, Denny's International named it one of the two top programs they'd done worldwide that year. And it continued on for years in other markets as well.

But right there in a nutshell is the beauty of sponsorships. We were able to affiliate Denny's with something the customers in their market loved – namely the San Diego Padres. It was targeted, intimate, not filtered-out—and very, very effective.

So let me ask you, why can't you do something like this for — and with — the companies in your market?

Simply stated, you can.

And if you follow the rules as outlined in the chapters that follow, you'll soon be doing *exactly* that; Helping the businesses in your "world" to tap into your customers, clients, readers, and followers, doing your people a solid service and helping your bottom line immeasurably.

As the sign on the door says: Welcome to the "Wild, Wild World of Sponsorship." Buckle up... I think you're going to enjoy the ride!

Chapter Three

"The Is's... and Isn'ts of Sponsorship"

So Far, So Good

To this point, you should now have a good idea of what sponsorship is…as well as the fact that there are literally billions of dollars being invested each and every year by companies looking to affix their name to various programs and properties out there.

So far, so good.

That done, let's start now by trying to rope this in a little bit and bring it down from the national stage to your specific property. How can you take this information and apply it to your association, group or upcoming boot camp?

Selling and Servicing Your Sponsors Isn't EASY … but It Is Pretty SIMPLE

I'm not going to lie to you and say it will be easy. It won't. But I will tell you that it's going to be fairly simple.

And it starts by recognizing and realizing what sponsorship is—and also what it isn't.

- **Sponsorship ISN'T a "money grab."** Nobody worth their salt is going to do you a favor here and hand you a whopping check for the right to hang a banner up in the front of your meeting room. That's not going to happen, so get any "get rich quick" notions out of your head right now.

Sponsoring you—or not sponsoring you— is strictly a business decision, nothing more. It's a company (or companies) looking at the assets you bring to the table and deciding if they can derive some business from tapping into those assets.

- **Sponsorship IS a relationship business.** If you're going to be any good at this, it'll be because you quickly realize that you're going to need to start to care as much about your sponsors as you do about your existing customers.

(In fact, do this right and your sponsors will become your BIGGEST customers!) Perhaps a little bit differently than the folks sitting out there in your audience, but customers nonetheless. And like anything worth pursuing, your sponsors are worth keeping. Let's face it, it's not going to do you a whole lot of good if you bust your tail to get a handful of sponsors on board if they keep bailing out at the end of your contract!

The Key Is Getting into THEIR Business... and Out of Your OWN

So you're going to have to learn to take care of them. Take good care of them.

Care about what they care about and take time to learn as much as you can about their business and how it relates to your customers. It's a fact; the more you can help these sponsors do what they need done to effectively reach your customers, the more they're going to like it, and the greater the value of their sponsorship with you will be.

This relationship-building process is a problem I see happening time and time again. (And by people who should know better!) They knock themselves out trying to wine and dine their sponsors in an effort to get them on board. But once that's done, they're moving on to the next one. Once the first signs the contract, they tend to pretty much completely forget about them. Yes, they hang their signs and execute their promotion, but, for the most part, they make little or no effort to stay in touch with their sponsors. At least not until the year's up and it's time for the renewal. Then it's "George, my best friend, how's it going?"

Trust me, sponsors can see through that like a one-ply towel! And they hate it.

Sponsorship Done Right

Here's an example of sponsorship done right: NASCAR, which is amazingly popular with corporate America. NASCAR was pretty much built around sponsorship, and they've never forgotten it. From the drivers in the Pepsi car to the owners along pit row and the managers at Lowe's Motor Speedway, it's a case of "In Sponsors We Trust!"

And take a good look at any one of those suped-up Chevys! You won't find that many logos in the phone book!

And only slightly less covered in corporate insignia are the drivers themselves—and only because there is less of them to cover than there is on their car!

There's a mantra in NASCAR that goes: "Win on Sunday—sell on Monday!" Every driver on the track knows that turning left at 189 miles an hour is only *one* of their responsibilities.

In racing, it's not just about winning races. It's about being "one with your sponsors" and helping them to leverage their investment in you and your driving team. And the drivers are more than happy to do their part. As soon as Sunday's race is over they're out on the highway heading down to the next weekend's race locale. They'll pull into Charlotte or Daytona literally days before the race so that they can do some "meet 'n' greets" with their sponsor's key customers or get into the area grocery stores to sign some boxes of the sponsor's cereal.

Their legions of fans love them. And, because they love them, they're only too happy to buy the products that support their favorite drivers. It's a thing of beauty and a lesson that all of us in sponsorship should learn.

In short, the key to successful sponsorships is successful relationships. In over 25 years of selling packages, I can honestly tell you I've never had so much as a single company buy a sponsorship from me. Never happened. Never will. But I've had hundreds of *people* buy them from me. And it's keeping those people and their needs forefront in mind that's helped us to sell—and *re*-sell—those sponsorships year…after year…after year.

Banner Hanging Is for Beginners— You're BETTER Than That!

- **Sponsorship isn't just about hanging a banner or running an ad in your program.** This is another problem I see cropping up all too often—mostly among folks new to the sponsorship game. To them, sponsorships are pretty basic: hang up a banner or mention them a few times from up on stage and you've pretty much done all you can do, right? WRONG!

You'll be amazed at how much you can do to help your sponsors get out—and stay out—in front of your customers. One of the things that separates "traditional advertising" from sponsorships is that advertising is pretty much about exposure—getting your name out in front of target market customers. Sponsorship, on the other hand is about that, and then some. Sponsorships are about "touches" and enabling your sponsors to literally get out there and meet their customers face-to-face in a non-threatening, non-commercial environment. This is why oftentimes the mark of a good sponsorship isn't necessarily in the quantity of consumers they get exposed to, but in the quality and frequency of those touches.

So go ahead and hang up those banners, but, in the pages to come, we're going to start exposing you to some ways that you can help your sponsors to *really* tap into your customers and attendees. And it's in that quality and frequency that you're going to discover the real value to your sponsorships!

It's a MARATHON...Not a Sprint!

- **Most of all, Sponsorship is a MARATHON, not a SPRINT.** Let's finish our sponsorship "is and isn'ts" with this one. It's frankly one of my favorite ones and one I use in every sponsorship class I teach.

Most folks diving into sponsorship sales are literally chomping at the bit. Once they see the money that is to be had from selling sponsorship to their group or property, they're like a kid in a candy store! They're out there sending proposals to every company they can to try to fast talk them into a fast deal. And for the most part, they're failing miserably.

So let me slow you down a tick here. If you're going to truly get the sponsor mindset, you're going to recognize that sponsorship sales is a marathon—not a sprint. If you get into it, get in it for the long haul.

Having done as much as I have in selling sponsorships, I get approached by many companies interested in having me consult for them on selling sponsorships. I've got to tell you, for the most part, I'm happy to have this discussion with them, but I warn them right up front, I'm not cheap. As of this writing, our going rate is $10,000 a month retainer plus 15% of what we sell.

That information is enough to usually have them leaving skid marks getting off the phone. But if they're still on the line, I then caution them that sponsorship isn't another word for "quick cash." I tell those companies interested in hiring me that sponsorship is very much a "Ready…Aim…Fire!" proposition:

"Ready…" *The process starts by learning about your client. What do they do, what do they have (their "assets"), and who would want to tap into your new client's assets. What are the unique benefits this new client can offer outside companies, and so forth?*

"Aim…" *Once you know as much as you can about your new client and their assets, it's time to start looking for some matches.*

"Fire!" *Once you know what you've got, and put together a target list of prospects that might have an interest in tapping into those assets, it's time to go out there and pursue it.*

Sponsorship is all about timing–bringing the right offer to the right people at the right time. Miss any one of those three ingredients and you'll come away empty-handed.

The Sales of Sponsorship

No matter how you slice and dice it, sponsorship is about sales. But, take heart; even if you don't think of yourself as a sales person, you can do this!

Selling sponsorship is oftentimes about developing persistence and patience. It's not necessarily about being a "good salesperson." It's about having the right temperament.

In the sports world I tend to meet all kinds of sales people: Men, women, eager young pups, and seasoned veterans of the sales wars.

But as different as they all are, I tend to notice that they seemingly come in one of two types:

"TYPE A" SALESPEOPLE

These are the "quick hitters" out there—and they invariably don't do particularly well at sponsorship sales. Not that they're not nice people or good at sales—many of them are. But Type A's tend to be impatient. They want results—and they want results now! And that's not generally conducive to an effective sponsorship sales executive.

Type A's tend to make great ticket salespeople in my world. For them, sales are very much a numbers game and they know how to play the percentages. Get 'em in and get 'em out is their mantra and they're amazing to watch! I like to tease my "Type A" buddies because you can't help but notice that they tend to drive fast sporty cars dress in the hottest trends and drum their fingers a lot!

THE "TYPE B" SALESPEOPLE

Type B's on the other hand are built for endurance climbs. They don't generate nearly the sales activity that their Type A counterparts do, but in the end, their dollars oftentimes wind up several times the size of their compatriots.

Where the Type A's are all about the numbers, Type B's tend to live by the adage that "Life is about the journey—not the destination!" The good Type B's are often very meticulous and quite personable. They want to make friends, not just generate customers. And they don't drive sports cars, they drive luxury cars. With big leather seats and a great stereo.

If it sounds like I tend to prefer Type B's, it's probably because I am one! But I mean Type A's no disrespect. Fact is, I tried being a Type A and quickly discovered that I was lousy at it. However, I'm smart enough to recognize that in order to be successful; you've either got to have either some Type A in you or around you. I've found that Type A's are the hard-driving folks that keep pushing to get things done, and you've got to have that as you get your business up and off the ground.

So if that's you, and you're used to covering a lot of ground quickly, you might need to re-wire a bit for selling sponsorships. Instead of an "in or out" mentality, seek to develop more patience, work on your relationship development skills and give yourself more time to bring those big sponsors aboard. Sponsorship is still a "numbers game," but the sales cycle is invariably longer. Just know that the results invariably make it worth the wait.

Chapter Four

"Sorry, But They REALLY Don't Care About You..."

Okay – It's Painful Truth Time

What's driving you, and most other meeting, organization and event planners into delving into the world of sponsorship, is an overwhelming desire to balance your bottom line or even to make a couple of extra pesos on your upcoming event or boot camp. Maybe you read an article out there that mentioned that not too long ago down in Texas, the Houston Texans NFL football team convinced Reliant Energy to spend $12 million a year, for the next 20 years, to put their name on the Texans new stadium.

"Sheesh," you're thinking, "if someone out there is open to dropping a quarter of a billion dollars to carve their name up on a building surely I can find someone who will spend $5,000 to sponsor my association, right?"

Well, the simple answer to that is: "Yes," "No," and "It depends."

It depends on who you talk to, what they need, and what you've got to offer them in return. The key is to never forget that corporate America doesn't care about what YOU want or what YOU need. They really and truly only care about one thing. They care only about what *they* want.

To capture their kimchi, you're going to have to be willing to completely change your thinking. It's no longer about you or your event or your monetary needs. From this point moving forward, sponsorship is going to now become about *their* needs, *their* objectives, *their* goals and your ability to help them to accomplish those goals.

Sponsorship tends to mirror every other business out there in that supply exceeds demand. This is as true in the number of fast food restaurants open today as it is in the number of opportunities to sponsor different properties, meetings and events. The plain truth is that companies today are literally inundated with sponsorship opportunities, and yours is just one more making it's way out there somewhere onto a large and ever-growing pile.

Which is why it's important, if you're going to have success doing this, that you need to understand what goes on over on the sponsor's side of the table. Or, as a fisherman buddy of mine once told me, "If you wanna catch a fish, you've gotta learn how to THINK like a fish!"

With that said, and your pole firmly in the water, we're going to take a couple minutes here to take you inside the minds of your "fish."

Insider Insight: "The Nifty Fifty"

Starting back in 1995, and then every two years afterwards, our organization, The National Sports Forum has undertaken (with the outstanding and much-appreciated assistance of the Ohio University Center for Sports Administration), an extensive study called *The NSF Corporate & Industry Survey*. The crux of this biannual report is an in-depth interview process we conduct with fifty of the top corporate sports sponsors and advertisers in the United States.

Our survey people spend literally hours with these top check writers gaining their insights as to the "state of sports sponsorship." Our interest is to learn who is doing it right and, more importantly, what does "doing it right" mean to these top executives? What are the things today's sponsors want to see in their sponsorship programs? And what are the elements they're seeing that they really don't care about?

Each interview takes about 60-90 minutes to conduct and over the years, we've added some new questions and deleted others. But one question that's always stayed the same has been our last question: "If you could tell all the people out there trying to sell you sponsorships and advertising packages one thing—the one thing that could help them—and help you—be more successful in their endeavors, what would that one piece of advice be?"

Over the years this has proven to be a great last question as it gives our "Nifty Fifty" a chance to wrap everything they've talked about up in one fell swoop. We've come away with some outstanding advice and recommendations, which we then present every other year at the Sports Forum as well as offer it up in a series of webinars.

The THREE Things Companies Want You to Do BEFORE You Walk Through Their Door

The reason I mention this question is that the number one complaint put forth by our "Nifty Fifty" is every bit as viable in the meeting and association industry as it is in theirs. It's a cardinal sin one need take great pains not to fall into and that is: Don't fall in love with your *own* business, fall in love with *theirs*.

Here are a couple samples of what our "Nifty Fifty" told us....

- **"Do your homework;** learn as much as you can about my business before you come in here. And look for opportunities where you can make an impact on my bottom line."

- "I'd tell them to **visit us and learn our business.** Come to our house. Walk the walk."

- **"Take a fresh approach** and act like a company that wants to help us build our business as opposed to a company that wants to sell us 'fixed items' to help them meet their budget."

The bulk of the survey, as you might imagine, pertains to sports-centric benefits and properties, but there are sponsorship "true-isms" that are just as valid in one world as they are in another.

Another question from our biannual corporate survey gives you a taste of how rapidly the field of sponsorship is growing out there. The question we asked was, "In a typical week, how many sponsorship proposals do you and your department receive?"

We only added this question to the survey a few years back with the *2006 Corporate Survey.* But already we've spied what we think is a coming "trend" from our corporate interviews discussing the tremendous influx of proposals they've been getting.

The sponsorship world out there has just exploded over the last 20 years, and with it has come an explosion in the number of teams, leagues, events, charities and organizations all looking for sponsorship dollars to help them to balance their budgets.

We thought that it might prove helpful to demonstrate to you the numbers of sponsor "competitors" you have out there by showing you the numbers of proposals our *2006 Corporate Survey* "Nifty Fifty" had come across their desks:

- In 2006, corporate sponsors reported receiving an average of **15.8 sponsorship proposals per week.**

- But just two years later, in 2008, Corporate America reported that this number had grown to the point where they're now receiving an average of **28.7 sponsorship proposals per week!**

- That's an increase of almost **82%** in just *two years* and comes to almost **1,500 sponsorship proposals crossing their desk every year!**

Getting From the "B-pile"...Into Their "A-pile"

As you might imagine, that's a lot of reading—particularly for busy executives who don't have "review sponsorship proposals" in their job descriptions! That results in a ton of extra work for these busy and stretched executives who are already juggling a million other marketing and sales duties in their schedules. Should come as no surprise that many a "Nifty Fifty-ite" has expressed a desire to have someone on staff that had nothing else to do but read and evaluate all of the sponsorship proposals that come in every week!

But what does this mean to you? Particularly since you'll most likely be going after more local sponsors and not the national corporations?

Well, whether it's on the local level, or the national level, what it means is that you're going to run into some competition out there—lots of it!

It also means that if you're going to break through all the traffic out there, you're going to have to do your homework. You're going to have to quickly and concisely identify your "audience" to your prospects. And lastly, to be effective, as mentioned earlier, you're going to have to fall in love with your prospect's business/industry instead of just your own.

But if you can do all that, and we'll show you how, you're going to discover how to successfully put together the kind of proposal that gets your property considered and gets your proposal switched from the "B" pile, over to the "A" pile, and then on into the "Done" pile.

With that said, go ahead and stretch your legs, refill your coffee and then let's get down to work. We're going to spend the next couple chapters explaining to you exactly how to do all of the above. Ready?

Chapter Five

"Say...What'da ya Know...?"

Let's Start Off with a Quick Question

As a meeting owner, conference organizer, bootcamp impresario or even a newsletter publisher—what's the best, most valuable thing you've got?

Is it your organizational skills, your stellar writing style or your razor sharp negotiation talents? Ummm...no, no, and nope.

What's the Best, MOST VALUABLE Thing You Own in Your Business?

Not to downplay any of your adept developmental skills, but quite frankly, the best, most valuable thing you "own" is your database— your customer list. Fact is, tomorrow morning the government could swoop in and take everything you own, but so long as you hang onto your database of loyal steady customers, you can get it all back, and then some, in a relatively short period of time.

It's this roster of readers, customers, current and past clients, former attendees, on-going association members and, even to a certain extent, some of your hottest prospects that comprises your "herd" and it should be guarded and treasured like the gold in Fort Knox.

For it's this herd of yours that is going to keep you in business, and it's this very same group that is going to get you noticed by the legions of potential sponsors out there.

Not to confuse this with some easily bought database of mailing list names, your herd is far beyond that. What you've managed to build up over time is a vibrant, invaluable, growing roster of people who are partial to doing business with you. They believe in you and have demonstrated with their hard-earned money their belief in your products or services.

Don't take that lightly and whatever you do, don't ignore your herd.

I've had over the years the good fortune to have learned from a number of outstanding mentors, many of whom I've never even met. Great authors, great teachers and great leaders, all of them. And one of the best for me is a man by the name of Dan Kennedy, who actually coined the term "herd." Over the years, I've listened to Dan on CD, read his books, watched him on video, subscribed to his newsletters and even seen him up on stage, but actually, at least to this point, I've not yet met him. But that hasn't stopped me from gaining a lot of knowledge from him.

And one of the many things I've learned from my time on "Planet Dan" is the value of building a fence around your herd. He counsels that most businesses out there think their only goal in getting a customer is to make a sale. But once you really get it, you see that the real value of making a sale is to get a customer.

For once you get a customer, you can go back to these folks time and time again to deliver more value, more information and sell them more of your products and services. That's, indeed, what Dan does. (He's done that to me! I can tell you that over the years I've invested thousands of dollars in his products and never once regretted a dime of it.)

But Dan didn't just come to me once, make a sale and move on. No—he grew me, cultivated me and turned me into an on-going customer. And you should do likewise.

Not just because maintaining a relationship with your customers is good for your direct sales, (via repeat business)... it's also good for your sponsorship efforts. Your greatest asset will be your roster of loyal customers. Because that, more than just about anything, is what will get your prospects' attention. Being able to tap into your herd to promote their goods and services is well worth the price of admission to the right roster of prospect. But to gain their interest, and their business, you have to be able to accurately describe and promote your herd to these prospective sponsors.

What do you KNOW About Them?

So let me start by asking you, what exactly do you know about your herd—in this case the people who support your business?

Maybe you know their names, their addresses, possibly even their e-mail addresses? However, for many of you, you might be admitting to yourself that you really have no clue as to who your customers are!

Don't be chagrined. Fact is, most companies haven't any idea who their customers are.

They'll think nothing of spending hundreds, thousands, maybe even millions of dollars buying mass-market advertising to get folks through their doors. But once they're there, they won't take ten minutes to find out who they are! Frankly, this never fails to amaze me.

Find Out Who They Are – If you're not capturing your customer information, start right now! And not just their names and addresses. Short of employing the third degree; get as much information as you can. Maybe not all at once—start with just a few basics, but over time, every time they call in or order online, shoot them a follow-up "getting to know you" question. Keep filling in your customer profile, keeping in mind that the more you know, the more valuable your database is.

As you start to gather and put your core customer, member, attendee information together, you start building your customer profile. Your typical customer profile is a composite average of all of the information you've gathered that when boiled down gives you a very fair picture of who your typical customer is.

Researchers tend to boil this information down into primarily two different "pools" of information:

DEMOGRAPHICS

Demographics refer to selected population characteristics of your customers (members, attendees, patrons, participants, etc.) Commonly-used demographics include such things as race, sex, age, income, disabilities, mobility (in terms of travel time to work or number of vehicles available), educational attainment, home ownership, employment status, and even location.

PSYCHOGRAPHICS

Psychographics on the other hand are a "deeper dive" on your customers. Whereas demographics tell you *who* your customers are, where they live and so forth, psychographics tells you more about *what* they believe in. Attributes relating to personality, values, attitudes, interests, or lifestyles are all divided through psychographic questions. Along with this, you'll gain insights into your customers' behavior patterns, social mores and lifestyle choices.

Start by getting the simple things: your customers' demographics. Just being able to gather demographic information and present that to your prospective sponsors is a decided plus. You can begin by putting the information together in "snapshots" to present to your prospective sponsors.

For instance, let's suppose you oversaw an association focused on the chiropractic community. You could put together snapshots broken down as follows:

- **Member Qualifications** – What percentage of your association members are the chiropractic doctors themselves? Their assistants? Physical therapists? X-ray techs? And so on.

- **Geographic Background** – Where do your association members practice? What percentage is from the north, the east, the southwest, etc. (This information could prove very important for a sponsor that matches up well geographically with a large segment of your association members.)

- **Size of Practice** – What percentage are single doctor practices and what percentage are multi-doctor? How many employees do they have? How many patients, on average, do they treat per day?

- **Services Offered** – What percentage specialize in certain injury treatments? What percentage offer physical therapy? How many offer any other services beyond basic chiropractic treatment, and what are these services?

- **How Long Have They Been in Business** – What chunk of your attendees are mature, developed practices and what percentage are start-ups?

- **What Problems Are They Facing** – This is always a great question to ask your herd. With problems there are invariably solutions—and companies eager to provide those solutions. Armed with the 10-12 major problem areas your members are wrestling with you can now set about the task of searching out those companies, agencies, solution-providers that would have strong interest in servicing your association members. These make up potential sponsor candidates.

- **What Are They Looking for From Your Association –** Another good question to run by your members. What's driving your members to join your association anyway? Are they looking for strong sales training? Marketing? Office operations? Management? New treatment education? Certification?

Why is this information valuable? Say, for instance, one of the hottest hot buttons driving the doctors to join your association is their desire to latch onto the latest in patient retention techniques. In that case, spending a lot of time trying to pitch sponsorships to new equipment manufacturers, while not a complete waste of time, might not resonate with your association members as readily as getting a printer or Internet marketing company on board as a sponsor. Your sponsors' offerings and your audience wants should be as close a match as you can get.

Hopefully this serves to give you a pretty good idea of the type of information you're looking to gather. If so, you're now ready for your next "Homework Assignment."

Homework Assignment: *This one's a quickie, and, best of all ... there are no right or wrong answers!*

Left hand side: On the left hand side I want you to put together a list of what you think the demographic profile of your customers looks like. Give this some thought and write down some of the basics...

Right hand side: What are some of the general characteristics of your herd? Give yourself some free-thinking space to jot down some of the things you come up with...

Demographic Profile

Sex – What percentage of your herd is male? Female?

Age Range – What percentage fall somewhere between 21-30? 31-40? 41-50? Over 50 years of age?

Income – What percentage of your customer base makes less than $35,000 annually? Between $35K-$60K? Between $60K-$80K? Between $80K-$100K? Over $100,000 annually?

White Collar vs. Blue Collar – What are the job categories?

Education Level – College? High School? Special Training? Advanced Degrees?

Titles – Depending on your association or group, what percentage own the business? What percentage are vice presidents? Directors? Below director?

Another way to look at this, what percentage can make the buying decision, and what percentage has to run it up the chain of command?

General Characteristics

What do they spend their money on – What are some of the basic things they all tend to need for their businesses? Medical or office insurance? Office supplies? Websites? Signage? Transportation? Overnight shipping? Catering?

Go deep here. You can use the entire right hand side of the page but give yourself an extra line after each of these generalities.

How much – Once you finish jotting down the spending commonalities of all of your attendees, go back now and make some notes bracketing what you "guess-timate" your typical member spends each year on each of these commonalities.

For instance, let's say that you oversee an association of chiropractors and—after completing this exercise you "uncover" that one of the common needs of your group is printing, and that you have 200 members in your association.

(You might want to break out a couple extra sheets of paper for this part, but that's okay—it's worth the investment!)

As you start giving this some thought, you estimate your members need to print up such things as medical pads, promotional calendars, monthly patient newsletters, business cards, brochures, and special treatment pamphlets every year. All told, it's not beyond the realm of possibility that each of your members spends between $20,000-$25,000 a year on printing.

Let's pick a realistic middle amount of $23,000 and do the math...

200 members x $23,000 = $4.6 million

That's a pretty impressive number, don't you think? And while you're at it, don't you think Acme Speedyprint might have an interest in tapping into over $4.5 million worth of printing? You bet they do! Good, you're starting to catch on now, aren't you?

Now go ahead and finish off the rest of the right hand column so that we can move on to the next piece of the puzzle, putting the target prospect list together!

Chapter Six

"Pilot to Bombardier"

Who's Interested in Buying
What You Have to Offer?

Hopefully by this point you're starting to get a little bit excited? Trust me, it's only going to get better because we've now reached the point where we can start to put together a roster of target prospects.

Let me start this exercise by sharing with you the number one question that invariably crops up every time I start talking sponsorship sales to folks with properties. Without fail someone in the first five minutes will turn to me and say, "But, who would want to sponsor me and my business?"

Well now, given that you've completed your homework assignment at the end of the last chapter, let me ask you that same question. Armed with what you now know, you should begin to visualize who might have an interest in stepping up and talking to you about sponsoring your group?

I think the two things that surprise people once they put together their roster of sponsor categories is first that there are literally entire categories of companies that would be interested in being approached on a sponsorship/advertising package. The second surprise is how many companies and categories there are out there to go after!

This is great because when you're done, you could easily have a dozen different sponsors all tapping into your herd and all happily paying you for this opportunity. Not that there isn't a saturation point on the number of sponsors you can effectively service, but we'll get into that later in this book. For now, let's start with getting the most important one—the first one!

Create a Sponsorship Hit List

Grab a pad of paper and go back to the homework assignment from the last chapter. You're going to need to go back to the left hand demographic information when you start drafting your initial proposals coming up, but, for now, we're going to focus on the possible sponsor categories.

Go back over the roster of purchasing commonalities that the majority of your members/ readers/attendees share and dedicate one page to each of the commonalities. In other words, in the case of the chiropractors association, one page would be titled "Medical Insurance," the next page might be titled "Printers," a third page could be titled "Vitamins/Supplements" and so forth.

Once done, your job will be to go back and fill in every page with companies that sell the services/products you've just written down. Be all inclusive, from the giant to the small; from the national to the regional. Your priority right now isn't to qualify your candidates; it's just to capture their names. We'll go back soon enough and start to pare the lists down. But for now, more is better!

_____

And here's a thought...

In almost every case out there, there's really no reason for you to do this alone. Why not take a page out of our book when we started the National Sports Forum (Sports Forum)? After trying to go it alone that first year, we quickly wised up and created a steering committee to help us with things such as connecting with us potential sponsors.

You might give some thought to doing the same thing. Invite a small core group of your active members--folks who are really "into" what you're offering and invite them to make up an advisory committee for your program. You'll be amazed at how valuable their insights and recommendations can be. Not just with things such as discussion topics and speakers, but also with possible sponsor categories and company introductions.

However, be it by yourself or with the help of an advisory committee, the goal here is to get writer's cramp! Keep filling up the pages and keep adding possible categories.

Where to Find Them

The Value of Magazines - Keep the steam coming by purchasing as many magazines as you can within your industry specialty. In fact, as mentioned above, one of the best questions you can ask your members, readers, and attendees when you're compiling your psychographic research is: "What industry magazines do you receive?" Those magazines have value from several angles. They are also an amazing source of valuable information. From industry specifics to industry size, knowing what's contained in magazines in your industry help you to look cutting edge smart.

Compile a roster of the magazines your herd reads and start subscribing to them—and actively reading them. Besides the articles, pay particular attention to who advertises in those magazines. And start thinking of them not only as advertisers, but target industries. It's not just the companies themselves, but the category their product/service falls into. You'll be surprised to discover you'll be adding lots of new category potentials with every industry magazine you subscribe to.

Let's start by helping you to source possible sponsorship prospects through the industry magazines out there. As you might imagine, these magazines are in the business of selling advertising. And to sell all that advertising space each and every month, they need to convince potential advertisers out there that they have what the advertiser wants.

How do they do that?

The same way you're doing it; they gather information to help them to make their case. And many of them spare no expense when it comes to gathering the background research, demographics and psychographics of their market. The information many of these magazines have put together on your market will be invaluable to you, especially those from magazines that most closely mirror your group.

Put together a list of closely-targeted magazines and reach out to them. Flip open the first few pages of each of these magazines. Usually somewhere right before or shortly after the table of contents, you'll find the magazine's editorial box. This box lists the editorial staff, from the publisher on down to the editors, reporters and staff assistants. It also lists the magazine's phone number, web site URL, mailing address and so forth. Scan this roster, and you'll invariably find a listing for the advertising department. Bingo! That's what you're looking for. If for some strange reason you don't find the advertising department listed there, just call the magazine's front switch board and ask to speak to the ad department.

Once you get a hold of the advertising department, ask them if they would send you a sales kit from their magazine. They'll be more than happy to do so.

Not only will these kits give you all kinds of interesting background information you can use in putting your sponsorship sales materials together, but you'll also get a chance to see their circulation numbers. How "big" is the universe that your group functions in?

You'll see readership demographic information on their readers, which you should pay close attention to as they mirror those of your members.

You may also see some one-sheets in their sales kit on upcoming special issues or sections that are coming up for that magazine, special sales promotions the magazine is offering, or interesting ideas you can use to increase your herd. That's good information for you to dial into as well. Magazines tend to track the hot topics going on in your industry. That being the case you might get some great session topics for your next meeting or upcoming newsletter.

And notice as well how much they charge for their ads. You might be surprised—ads aren't cheap! That can be especially true in industry-targeted publications, where the audience is more specialized. In fact, the more specialized and tougher to access the market, the more expensive their advertising tends to be.

It's good for you to have some reference as to what other advertising avenues cost out there in your industry. That will help you as you start to set your sponsorship pricing. Knowing what your competition has, what they offer, and how much they charge for it is almost like stealing the other team's playbook before you tee it up against them on Sunday afternoon!

Now in case you're starting to feel like getting this information is unfair or unethical — trust me, it isn't. After all, there's a very good chance that you might wind up doing some business with them. In fact, there's a very good chance that they might be interested in coming aboard as one of your sponsors. (You've got what they want—why wouldn't they be interested in tapping into your herd of potential subscribers?)

You might consider, as you start digging into the publication, about buying an ad to promote your upcoming boot camp in one of their issues. Or that what you're doing could very possibly be of interest to this publication's readers, and you might want to submit an article for publication. (Free publicity!)

And lastly, many of these magazines are only too happy to sell you their subscriber mailing lists. Depending on what your group specialty is, if there's a good match to what you're offering, you'd be crazy not to consider buying their subscriber lists! These lists represent potentially thousands of new members to you. Go for it!

NOTE: A lot of these lists can be readily cut into various and sundry sub-category lists which you can then purchase. Say, for instance, you only want the magazines subscribers who are located in your state or the four states in your geographic region. Not a problem, just ask for it. Most of these magazines, or their list brokers, can "slice 'n dice" these lists and sell you only what makes the best sense for you in what you're doing.

But you probably wouldn't even consider doing business with these different magazines if you didn't know what they had to offer you. So don't feel reluctant to ask them for their sales kits, they're as interested in reaching you as you are in reaching them.

Final note about industry magazines: Spend time going through each magazine's website. You're bound to find lots of interesting information about the publication, the issues, the audience, etc., by clicking through their website pages. And make it a practice, especially with the ones that fit your niche the best, and go back every month or so to pick up the latest updates. It'll be time well spent.

Magazines are another way of putting together potential sponsor target lists. Magazines are a great way to do this. And along that same wavelength, what with the age of specialized television channels out there are there any TV shows followed by your herd? This might be an option if your group is more activity specific, such as a golf association or a publication focusing on the joys of antique hunting. As more and more channels come on line, you're seeing that we're living in the age of specialization. There are shows out there that just show guys playing poker, others that give the latest new tips on cake decorating. If you like it, trust me, it's out there. And with the advent of new technology, we're only just starting to see the age of specialization. Which leads me to your computer and the Internet.

When it comes to building your prospective target list, the Internet is going to become your new best friend!

In the old days, you really had to do some digging to find prospects, but no more. Now thanks to search engines like Google and Yahoo!, you have only to type in some key search words and within seconds up will pop literally hundreds of thousands of sponsor possibilities within each category. Jot 'em down, pilgrim, and keep going.

Along the way I can promise you something unique and strange will start to happen. As your antenna goes up looking for new sponsors, you'll suddenly be amazed at how you start seeing more and more candidates popping up out there. All of a sudden they're all around you! Just keep that antenna up and keep filling out those rosters.

Here are questions I ask all of my consulting clients when it comes to developing prospect lists:

#1 "Who wants what you have?" – As you start to create your prospective sponsor rosters, this question should be forefront in mind. The answer to this question will only start to crystallize once you begin to recognize exactly what it is you have.

If I'd asked you this question at the beginning, you'd probably tell me you have "a bunch of folks that do or like (_____)". You'd be right, but that information isn't going to help anybody.

What do you really know about these people, your herd? From the general, such as how many there are, to the more specific, such as how advanced or developed they are or how long they've been in business. All of that information is going to help you to start to zero in on who else out there wants access to your herd? Who wants what you have?

#2 "Who benefits by you doing what it is you do?" – The first question is more client/reader/member focused. This question is more focused on you. And whereas the last question was focused on identifying companies that make money off of what your members do, this question is directed on discovering who makes money off of what YOU do.

Think about it for a second. Every time you put on a boot camp or hold a meeting some hotel or convention hall is renting you that room and charging you money, right? You're providing your attendees with coffee, maybe lunch or breaks; somebody is making money off of that.

If you have a larger meeting, you might have several sessions going on around your event. You need signage, yes? Banners up on the wall—that's costing you money. How about the printing for the programs, the name badges, the flyers, and handouts? The audio-visual company is hitting your pocketbook if you're using screens, microphones or LCD panel projectors.

How about the area hotels that are housing your attendees? The airlines that are flying them in? The rental car companies? Every time you hold a gathering, you do what it is you do, someone is profiting off of it.

Since they're making money off of you, why shouldn't they help you? (Actually, what they're really doing is helping you to help themselves.)

When it comes to business, the door should swing both ways, don't you think?

It will, but usually only if you ask it to.

I'm not suggesting that your suppliers should bequeath you ridiculous sums of money, but they should support your efforts. Even if it's just a program ad, nobody should be allowed to ride for free. Who benefits by you doing what it is you do?

Hot Doggin' It With the Padres

As I mentioned back in the early chapters, in my former life I was in charge of all of the San Diego Padres' promotions and sponsorships. I served as a bit of a one-stop shop: I scheduled them, sold them and then serviced them. And with the ever-escalating price of baseball free agents being what they were at that time (some things never change), I was always on the lookout for new sponsors and new sponsorship categories.

The search could be a difficult one. But sometimes, I've got to admit, the answer could be lying right there under my nose and I never saw it. This was one of those instances.

It was late August in the late 80's, and I was sitting there in the stadium shortly after our game with the Phillies got underway. I remember that year because the Phillies were bad, but we were worse! And with every painful loss I grew increasingly more-than-ready for the season to be over. But this being August, I knew I had an even bigger problem in store for me than suffering through bad baseball. August is often budget time for ball clubs, and what a headache that was!

I hated budget time because not only did I have to focus on the on-going season, but now I had to start giving serious thought to the next baseball season literally months down the road. Budget time meant I had to map out all of my intended promotions for the following year, including how much each event was going to cost the club down to the bottom dollar. And, on top of that, I also had to go "on record" in terms of predicting how much I intended to bring aboard that next year in the way of sponsorship dollars for each event.

How could I guess that? I didn't even know what I'd be having for dinner the next night, and here I was in a position where I had to predict what Company XYZ would agree to pay to sponsor our 4th of July fireworks show eleven months from that night!

(And speaking of Company XYZ, who would be my sponsors that next season?)

And what about new sponsors? Heck, I'd approached just about every possible sponsor there was out there to be hit, hadn't I?

To put it simply, I was feeling frustrated.

And it was right about then, as I was sitting there in the stadium that night paying almost no attention to the ball game, that these two gentlemen broke my train of thought as they wanted to get by me in order to get back to their seats.

They'd obviously just come from the concession stand because both of them were bearing hot dogs 'n beer. So I quickly moved my knees off to one side to enable these two gents to get past me. But, unfortunately, the first guy stepped on one of my feet and managed to lose a little of his beer on my shirt. His buddy just about landed in my lap—brushing his mustard-laden hot dog on me along the way. And that's when it hit me!

I had the beer company on board as a sponsor, but what about the hot dog? In all my years at the Padres, I'd never once thought to reach out to the hot dog company. In fact, I didn't even know who our hot dog supplier was!

So I bolted out of my chair and shot over to the nearest concession stand. After helping towel me off, the hot dog lady told me where the hot dogs came from, and the next morning, I was on the phone to the supplier.

I started by apologizing for allowing way too many years to go by, and in all that time, I'd never even thought to reach out and invite this man to show his support for the San Diego Padres.

As it turned out, I was phoning a company located in Los Angeles and the hot dog man quickly forgave me by first chuckling and then informing me "That's okay, we're Dodgers fans up here!"

I told him that we'd be only too happy to forgive him his obviously misguided selection of favorite teams, if he would consider sponsoring the San Diego Padres?

"No, no," he said, "We're all Dodgers fans up here, and we support the LA Dodgers. In fact, we've sponsored the ball club since they moved out west in 1958!"

I knew that and responded as such to my new friend. But I told him that I would take personal responsibility in making sure that his company would be as happy supporting the Padres as they have all these years in supporting the Dodgers.

"You don't seem to understand, son," (I loved it when they call me "son"...), "...but we have no interest in supporting the San Diego Padres—we only support the Dodgers."

"But wait a second, you sell your hot dogs to our fans down here at the stadium."

"That's right." he replied, "What's your point?"

"Well, I'm just curious; do you only sell your hot dogs to the Dodgers fans attending our games?"

"Noooo... (About now I could tell I was starting to tax his good nature...), we sell them to all the fans down there."

"Ohhh," I said, giving it my best drawn out Columbo-take, "let me see if I get this right. You only have interest in taking money from our fans, but not in showing any support or loyalty for what they believe in. Is that right?"

Well—that did it. Now he was cheesed off. "Look, son, you can slice this up anyway you want to but in the end, we're Dodgers sponsors, we've been Dodgers sponsors and we'll stay Dodgers sponsors. And that's it."

I retreated a little bit, but not really. "I'm sorry," I said. "I didn't mean to upset you, sir, and I see that I have. I'll let you go back about your business, but before I hang up I just wanted to say that I can only hope that Oscar Mayer is as loyal to us next season when they're selling their hot dogs in our stadium as you have been to the Dodgers."

The shot obviously hit home. "You can't do that!" he blustered.

"Oh, but I can," I assured him. "You need to look at your contract. There's a clause in there that gives this club the right of final approval on all of the suppliers used during our games."

And that was all it took.

We moved out of that stadium five years later on into a shiny new ballpark in downtown San Diego, but from that next season on until the year we played our final game at Qualcomm Stadium, that hot dog supplier owned one of the nicest tri-vision panels our ball club had to offer!

I'd probably still be tormenting him in the new stadium; however, I moved on shortly after that vendor's initial season with us. But the lesson here and the question I want to ask you is: who are your hot dog suppliers?

For instance, when we put on the Sports Forum, the city we take the conference to is required to pay us a sponsorship fee to bring our meeting to their city. On top of that, our host hotel pays us a fee to sell their hotel rooms to our attendees.

Frankly, if you're making money off of us, you should help feed the fire.

What I would encourage you to do right now before you move on and forget about this is to crack open your checkbook and start jotting down all of the suppliers that you write checks to.

Who are you supporting out there? And isn't it high time that they were, in turn, returning the favor and supporting you as well?

Creating your Sponsorship "War Room"

This is something we do with our sponsorship sales people at my agency when we're putting together category lists for our sponsorship clients. We call it creating our "Sponsorship War Room."

All you need to do to create your own Sponsorship War Room is to gather together all those prospective sponsorship candidate pads of paper and go out and purchase three things: a pack of 3" x 5" index cards, a black Sharpie pen, and six dozen thumb tacks. Armed now with your office supplies, return home and clear off one wall in your home/office. That's it; you're ready.

By now, your pads of paper are no doubt filled with what are hundreds of sponsorship candidates under the various categories. What we're going to do now is start to cull these lists. Also, by this time you've finished pouring through the Internet, jotted down all the magazine ads, and discussed category and candidate possibilities extensively with your ad hoc advisory committee. You're bound to now possess pads containing quite possibly several dozen lists of possible sponsorship categories. Great job—you've done well!

Separate and Categorize - As you start to review all of the varied categories you've created, one thing you'll start to notice is that some categories are going to jump out at you as being more naturals than other categories. For one thing, some categories are going to seem more universal to you than others (i.e. printers, office supplies, insurance, etc.) whereas others might be more finite in member appeal—meaning possibly that smaller sub-niches of your readers/members are impacted by this product/service, and so on.

That's okay, as you're initially putting your categories together, don't value judge at first. Just write them down and fill out the candidate possibilities as you go along.

Once that's done, and all your lists are filled out and all of your categories established, it's time to start paring things down.

Let's start the paring process by creating two overall folders—one containing the sheets of the more universal categories and the other folder housing all of the finite categories.

That done, let's begin with the more universal products/services. These are the first ones we're going to go after. Reason being that the more universal the target's products/ services are, the greater the number of your members who are going to be in need of those products/services. And the larger the number of interested members/readers/attendees who exist within your herd who are in the market, the greater your prospective sponsor's interest is going to be in getting out in front of your herd.

Not that there isn't gold to be mined in your finite categories, there is. But let's tackle the higher probability ones first and get things off the ground. Armed with your universal list, go through the rosters and select the 10-15-20 categories that, in your opinion, have the the highest amount of interest in getting in front of your herd.

Make It Visual - Take each category heading and with a black Sharpie, jot that title onto one of your 3"x5" index cards. Tape that header card as high up on your office wall as you can, leaving yourself plenty of room below the header card. Next up, go back to that category on your notepads and look at the roster of companies that you've written down that provide the product/service listed on your header card. Who knows—you might easily have 20, 45, 100 companies or more in any given category that are players in that product/service. Some are bound to be bigger players in that category than others. That doesn't necessarily make them better prospects than the smaller fish. In fact, you might soon find out that the bigger guys are too massive or too bureaucratic to have any interest in you or your group, and the smaller guys are more amenable, more flexible to approach.

What you're going to do now is go through your roster of category companies within that first selected category and start to rank your prospects within that given category. You're going to rank them in order of how strong a match you think they are and how receptive they might be to getting out in front of your group. Again, it's quite possible you might choose to rank a smaller firm ahead of a bigger company because the smaller firm has a larger overall interest in your niche or because they tend to concentrate on selling to your given niche that is located in your focused-upon geographic region.

You're going to discover right off the bat knowing what you already know about your industry, your area of concentration and your herd—that some companies are going to jump out at you as good prospects. Great, rank 'em high!

Looking over your roster, start by taking the top 10 ranked companies within that given category and jot the name of each company on a separate index card, one company name per index card. So that when you're done, you've now got ten index cards—each one containing the name of one of your top 10 prospects within that category.

Now break out your thumbtacks and post each index card, in ranking order, below the category header card. You should now have one long line of cards posted up on your wall.

Once you've finished with that initial category, go back to your lists and the second category. Take out that Sharpie pen and the index cards and start posting the next string of categories and candidates. Post them to the immediate right of your first string. And then the next, and so on.

When you're done, what you should have is a wall with 10 to 20 of the top universal category header cards along the top of the wall, with the top five-to-ten top ranked "target companies" below each header card.

You might be asking yourself why you have to write and post all of these out instead of just creating lists on pads of paper and stack them nice and neat right there on your desk. The answer is simple: you do this so that you'll get your sponsorships sold.

There's something so real about seeing everything laid out in front of you. You can't ignore it. Every time you walk in the office, there it is in front of you, prodding you to take action. And every time you complete an action with a given prospect, you break out your pencil, take down the card and jot down what you did. You do some background research on a given prospect, jot the date and what you did on the index card. You can write it on the back of the index card if you want to—the important thing is that you track your activity. If you get a contact name at the target company, for instance, write it down on the index card (name as well as phone number/e-mail address), so that way, if you misplace the information on your desk, it's right there on the card.

You send out a proposal, put it on your index card. You follow up, likewise. If you really want to land some sponsors, you have to get serious about it. So get serious about it! Track it so that I could walk into your office and know right off the bat what you're doing and where you're at with each one of your prospects.

Now go get 'em!

Chapter Seven

"What'll It Be, Mac?"

Discovering Your Assets and the Art of Creating Your Sponsorship Components

You've no doubt noticed by this point that I carved this book up into three separate sections, "Ready," "Aim," and "Fire!"

In the first few chapters I discussed the "Ready" portion of the sponsorship equation. Understanding what sponsorship is, how large it is, and its role in helping corporations and companies in their efforts to help get their names out into the public.

In "Aim," which is where I am now, I'm showing how to take your property and getting it ready to take its place as a sponsor-able entity. I start this section off by doing a deep dive into who your audience is and what they offer, as a herd, to the advertisers and sponsors out there.

In our last chapter, I took the next step and started fashioning together lists of specific categories, and companies within those categories, of prospects that would have an interest in tapping into your herd.

Selling Them What It Is They REALLY Want To Buy

So now you have the "what" and the "who," next up on the list is getting into the "how." As in how to take what you have and get it positioned to be purchased by a sponsor.

This is where things get interesting because here is where you get to start getting a little creative.

In this section you're going to learn how to recognize and break your property down into smaller sponsor-able entities that you will then combine in different packages to sell off to your soon-to-be sponsors.

Let's get this ball rolling by identifying a couple basic sponsor terms and its two subsets.

Access: What You're Offering - From a general standpoint, what you are first and foremost offering up to your field of potential sponsors is "access."

Access is just another term for granting permission, even helping, your sponsors reach out and touch your clients/customers/readers/members and so on. (For the sake of brevity, let's just keep calling them your herd.)

I suppose you could simply lump a bunch of companies together, call them your sponsors and stand up in front of your group that first morning and say: "Here's a roster of our sponsors...support them!"

That's pretty useless to your herd—and not going to do your sponsors a whole lot of good either.

Have you ever watched one of those televised sporting events when the announcer says, before the competition even begins, "This match is brought to you by Bob Jones' Sporting Goods, Acme Builders, and by your good friends at David's Lawn Care?" Ugh, how awful. You, the TV viewer, have forgotten those names before you even heard them! What good does that do anyone?

Instead, and here's where your creativity comes in, what would be better, more impactful, would be to weave your sponsors into the core fabric of your event. Give each of them ownership of different components of your event. Maybe even create a few components to your event that would allow your sponsors to have a presence, an identity, within your meeting, your convention, your boot camp, or even within your newsletter.

Identify Your Assets and Access - These components are frequently referred to, within the sponsorship industry, as being your assets. Taken as an official definition, assets are the identifiable components within your property that can be affiliated, associated and/or linked to the companies that are paying to be connected to your event.

So, in a nutshell then, what you're selling is access to your herd through your assets. Armed with those two terms, you're now ready to move forward.

The Two Assets You're Selling

Not to get too academic on you, but within the world of assets you're going to find there exists primarily two sub-sets of assets—tangible assets and intangible assets.

TANGIBLE ASSETS

Tangible assets are those components that can be seen, touched, felt—and can be readily measured. Let's give you a couple examples of what tangible assets might be.

Tickets - Let's say, for instance, you gave out or sold tickets to your conference or event. And on these tickets you printed your sponsor's name/logo on them. These tickets would then be a tangible asset. In other words, you have an asset. In this case, the tickets that have the name/tag line and/or logo of your sponsor on them, and this asset is something your attendees can see, touch, and feel. Can they be measured? Sure they can—you know how many of these tickets you put out into the market. So, sponsor-logoed tickets meet the criteria of a tangible asset.

Banners – If this is for a boot camp, you decided to print up a couple banners that recognized "Company XYZ" as the proud sponsor of your meeting. You've put that company's logo up there big and bold on both banners and hung one of them up by the main registration table so that everyone would see it when they first walked up to register for the camp. And you hung the other one up on the main stage.

Can you see, touch, and feel them? You only have to be able to do one of the three, and in this case, your attendees can definitely see them. And can they be measured? Yes again. You know how many attendees you have in attendance so you can quantify that the banners were seen by "x" number of attendees.

Here are some other things that would qualify as tangible assets:

- Sponsor name/logo imprinted on the cover of your *official program.*

- Sponsor inclusion on your printed *advance collateral* materials (ex. direct mail brochures, stationary, newsletters, and invitations).

- Mention of the sponsor on your *website.*

- *On-site product sampling* - Perhaps your sponsor has a product or service they can demonstrate or give-away at your boot camp.

- *Breakout session or panel inclusion* - Maybe you can get your sponsor involved in making a presentation or being part of a panel discussion at your boot camp. (This would have major value to a sponsor...)

- *Complimentary registrations* to your Boot Camp - Folding enough of these into your package so that your sponsor could not only come themselves as part of their sponsorship with you, but might also be able to bring potential key accounts or prospects of their own.

- *Trade show booth* - If you have a trade show component, giving them a booth in it as part of your package is a tangible asset.

- *Table Top Display* - Maybe you don't have a trade show running in conjunction with your boot camp, but because they're your sponsor, you'd set them up with a skirted 10-foot table in one corner and allow them the opportunity to set up samples of their products or demonstrations of their services and encourage your attendees to stop by.

- *Public Recognition* - Any occurrence where you stand up and either audibly or visually recognize your sponsor for their contribution to helping to make your meeting possible is a tangible asset. A great place to do this is up on the video screen in front of the main meeting room. Having your sponsor's logo up there on the screen before the main sessions start—either standing alone by itself or running it as a graphic in conjunction with the logo for your meeting—is a plus.

- *Name Badges & Lanyards* - This is another often-overlooked tangible benefit. Help cement the affiliation of one of your sponsors by including their logo on your name badges (tuck their logo in one of the corners), or imprint their name on the name badge lanyards.

- *On-site Promotional Giveaways* - At a lot of meetings the attendees are presented with a special commemorative notebook and/or pen to help them in their quest to take notes during the meeting. Be sure to have these sponsored and include the logo of one of your sponsors on the giveaways.

- *Coffee Breaks* - Have a couple signs set up on easels during coffee breaks that let your attendees know that the coffee break is compliments of one of your sponsors. Signage is very much a tangible benefit.

- *Room Key Cards* - Again, the key is to get creative, and this is one such example. Meetings are oftentimes held in hotels with the attendees, generally speaking, staying at that hotel. Most of the hotel rooms these days are electronically controlled, with the hotel giving you a credit card looking piece of plastic when you check in. Approach the hotel ahead of time and ask for permission to print up the hotel key "blanks" that will be given away to all of your attendees when they check into the hotel. (At the Sports Forum, we charge $13,500 for this component alone.)

- *Pre-Meeting Interview* - Do up an informational interview with one or more of your sponsors prior to your meeting or boot camp. What you do is spend a little time prior to the meeting interviewing them over the phone, record it, burn the interview onto a CD, and mail them out to all of your attendees a couple weeks before the meeting. **NOTE:** Make the topics you talk about relevant to what the meeting is about—these shouldn't be infomercials. Pick some topics for the conversation where you discuss a pertinent industry issue or problem and get your sponsor to explain how his/her company helps members solve those issues or problems.

- *Mailing List of Attendees* - This one isn't creative or clever, but just plain old common sense. That said, it's surprising how many meeting planners I run into who don't do this. Your sponsors are paying a premium to be involved with you—the least you can do is give them a run-down of not only who is attending, but how they can contact them. **NOTE:** Do this a couple times. Send your sponsors a roster/addresses of who you have signed up to participate a month or so out. Granted it's not a final list, as you'll undoubtedly have people signing up all the way to the last minute. By sending it out early, you're giving the sponsor the opportunity to do some advance marketing to your herd. They're able to promote their involvement with your event as well as talk a bit about their products/services. To this, they also can start to advance target those key prospects that they want to be sure to meet at your gathering. Then, right after the conference is over, send your sponsor a roster of everyone who attended. That way they can do some post-event marketing.

That's a taste but by no means a complete run-down of the types of different measurable tangible benefits out there. Use that list as a way to prime the pump to get you thinking of the ways that you can get your sponsors out there in front of your attendees. The more, the better. And the better you do, the more you can charge for it in return. Next up, intangible assets.

INTANGIBLE ASSETS

Intangible assets, or benefits, are those things you are able to offer to your sponsors that can't necessarily be measured or for that matter, can't necessarily even be purchased by an outside party.

The value of these benefits is oftentimes immeasurable. An intangible benefit, for example, might often take the form of something you are able to do for the sponsor, above and beyond the tangible things you can write, speak or say about them.

Let's take a shot at demonstrating for you a couple examples of intangible assets.

- *Official Affiliation with Your Event* - The very fact that you are partnering or affiliating your property with a sponsor is, in itself, an intangible asset. Without overtly or necessarily speaking a word, you are sending a message to your herd that this company is someone you have opted to do business with. The very act of your association is an implied endorsement of this company, and the more esteem in which your members hold you, the more valuable this asset is to your affiliating sponsors.

- *Right to Logo Usage* - Hand-in-glove with the official affiliation benefit is that of logo usage. One of the top intangible benefits your sponsors are granted is the right to use your logo in conjunction with their own in the promotion of their affiliation with your property. You'll see this a lot, for example, with US corporations that are "Official US Olympic Team Sponsors." They imprint the US Olympic logo next to their own on their print collateral, in-store, and on their TV commercials. Their spot might not even have anything to do with the US Olympic Team, but they put it on their materials anyway, because they know that to a lot of Americans, if you're the kind of company that supports the US Olympic Team, you're the kind of company that I want to do business with.

- *Exclusivity* - This is a big intangible asset, the right to be the only company in their category officially affiliated with your property, such as the official soft drink of such-and-such team or the official bank or credit card of so-and-so league. Having category exclusivity might not seem like much to you, but believe me, being able to block your competition from being able to get a foothold into your herd can be, depending on the property, one of the most valuable assets to be gained out in the sponsorship world.

- *Preferred Location* – For those events that contain a trade show component you know that success or failure in the trade shows can oftentimes be all about real estate. How well you do at the show, what kind of foot traffic your booth gets, who the other exhibitors are around you all have lots to do with where in the trade show hall you wind up. Talk to any trade show veteran, and they'll tell you, it's all about "location, location, location!"

NOTE: A tangible benefit is getting a booth in the trade show hall. An intangible benefit is where you get the trade show booth in the hall!

For us at the Sports Forum, when the trade show floor grid first comes out for the upcoming year's show, well before we release it to anyone, we block out and put a hold on all of the best booth locations in the hall. These spots are exclusively reserved for our sponsors. You want one, you have to become a sponsor of the Sports Forum. It's that simple. What's a benefit like this worth? Hard to say—it could be priceless depending on how well you do at the upcoming show.

- *Preferred Seating* – For those of you who don't have trade show components to your meetings, and even for those that do, you might want to seriously consider setting aside some preferred seating exclusively for your sponsors in the main hall. Maybe it's the front row center, like they do with rock concerts!

Anything that sets your sponsors apart from the masses is a plus mark in your column. Trust me, it doesn't go unnoticed by your sponsors. Nor does it pass unnoticed by others that might subsequently choose to become one of your sponsors.

- *Meet & Greets* – Here again is an intangible asset that brings smiles to the faces of your sponsors. Especially if you've got a celebrity-type speaker involved in your meeting, set up a special side room where either prior to the celebrity's presentation, or immediately afterwards, your sponsors are invited in for a private meet 'n greet with this noteworthy individual.

Because this is not something anyone other than those you invite could attend, for love or money, its value is completely intangible.

- *Right of First Renewal or a Right of First Refusal* – Again, not something that you could put a price on, but something that is highly valued in the right situations. At the Sports Forum, for instance, we grant a limited "right of first renewal" to our existing sponsors. Under this right, our existing sponsors have a set period of time, usually a two-month window of time immediately following the final year of their contract, when they have an exclusive opportunity to discuss sponsorship renewal with us. During that window, we don't solicit nor do we discuss that sponsor's inventory with anyone other than our current sponsor. In this way, our sponsors don't have to worry that we'll sell their program out from underneath them.

Somewhat similar to the "right of first renewal" is the "right of first refusal" option but be careful in offering that one up. A right of first refusal, unless it contains wording within the clause outlining specifics to the contrary, is something that, if not clarified, can work to your disadvantage.

By it's definition, a first refusal clause requires that once your contract expires on a program with your existing sponsor, should someone else surface wishing to pick up that piece of inventory, you would first be obligated to run it by your expired sponsor before you can sign a deal with someone else.

Furthermore, a lot of times a first refusal clause contains language that obligates you to offer the same deal at the same price and configuration to your just-expired sponsor as the one you're offering up to the potential new sponsor. There may be extenuating circumstances behind the deal you're offering up to the new sponsor that aren't in place with your expired sponsor. Just be careful on this one.

Now that you have a pretty good idea of the two types of assets you have to offer up, it's time for you to get to work.

Sponsorship Components

Break out those pads of lined paper, and let's get started by dissecting all of the various components of your event from beginning to the end. First thing I want you to do is put one of the below-outlined headlines at the top of each page of lined paper:

Pre-Event Print Collateral

Pre-Event Advertising

Website

On-Site Collateral

Official Program

On-Site Signage

On-Site Programs

Intangible Assets

Next up, take each one of these headlined pages and start to jot down the specific components you're going to be able to offer up to potential sponsors.

Let me take each header from the above list and get your thought processes going by giving you some specific examples of the types of program elements that go into each one.

Pre-Event Sponsorship Components

- **Pre-Event Collateral** – We talked about pre-event collateral in greater depth a bit earlier in the chapter, but as its name attests, what you want to jot down on this page are all the things you're either doing now, or could be doing in the future, that could include or incorporate your sponsor's name and/or logo.

Examples of sponsor-able pre-event collateral could include:

Event Letterhead – For instance, each year at the Sports Forum we're officially hosted by a different city in the United States. That being the case, we put the logo of that city's sports commission or convention & visitors bureau on our letterhead. We use that letterhead starting seven months prior and for the five months following our January conference to promote our sponsoring city.

Conference Brochures – No doubt, be it a boot camp, an association meeting, convention, conference, or seminar ... you have some written literature, such as a brochure, that tells your current and prospective members/clients/customers that your event is coming. Many of you have several advance pieces that you put out. Whatever you do, don't forget to include recognition of your event sponsors in your brochure.

Postcards – Again a natural for including the logos and recognition of your sponsors.

Newsletters – Many of us put out newsletters to our herd. It's a great practice to get into and something you should seriously consider doing if you're not doing one already. Not only does it serve to keep you front and center in front of your current customers, but it also affords you a marvelous opportunity to get in some recognition for your sponsors. Drop a story into one of your issues that welcomes your new sponsors into your sponsorship family, telling your readers who they are, what they do, and what their involvement in your upcoming event will be.

E-zines – This is a variation on the newsletter concept and helps keep you out not just in front of your existing herd, but also is a great entrée of your product/service to potential outsiders. At the Sports Forum, we do both a quarterly alumni newsletter as well as a biweekly e-zine. In every issue of our e-zine, "Selling It...", we include a box that contains special recognition of one of our various sponsors, partners or platinum vendors.

- **Pre-Event Advertising** – In some cases, you might have money set aside to purchase some traditional advertising to promote your upcoming event. (Magazine ads, newspaper, radio, and TV in some cases.) Make sure you set aside some space to include the logos of your sponsors.

- **Website** – In this day in age, who doesn't have a website for their upcoming event or property? It's invaluable for you, but don't forget that it's valuable real estate for your sponsors. Not only should you get their logos included in a special "salute to our sponsors" box on your home page, but it would also be a prudent move to have a special "about our sponsors" page to your web site. On that page, dedicate at least a paragraph to each of your sponsors. To this, be sure to include the sponsor's logo and name, but also a contact name, phone number, and e-mail should one of your web visitors wish to reach this company. Below the pertinent information on your sponsor, include a paragraph or so describing what that sponsor's company does and how his/her products or services can be a benefit to your audience. And lastly, if there's a special member's only incentive, such as a special white paper report or a member's only discount to be had, include that in the write up on each sponsor as well.

On-Site Sponsorship Components

- **On-Site Collateral** – In a moment we're going to talk about the official program, which just about all meetings or conferences have to some extent. But this one is to make sure that you don't forget your sponsors on other pieces of literature that get distributed at your event. Maybe you take special on-site candid shots of your attendees throughout the conference—get the sponsor's logos on the frames. Or perhaps you have a special floor map of the trade show—get those logos on there!

- **The Official Program** – Here traditional sponsorship can take on the guise of traditional advertising. In other words, that means that your sponsors' packages should provide your sponsors with an ad in your official program. Depending on the level of their spend (and the sophistication of your program), the higher spending sponsors should get the premium spaces of inside front cover, back cover, inside back and so forth. At the Sports Forum our sponsors get four-color premium placement ads. Our "partners" and "platinum vendors" get smaller black and white half or quarter-page ads inside the guts of the program.

However, in addition to ads, it's a good idea to have a special feature within your program that recognizes your event sponsors as well.

- **On-Site Signage** – We've already talked about banners. Always good to produce nice big banners that recognize your sponsors. Place these banners in prominent locations throughout your show, (i.e. up on the main stage, a couple in your trade show hall, by registration, maybe out in the central foyer—if the hotel will accommodate you.) In past years (and this varies hotel by hotel), we've had gobo lights that shined the logos of our sponsors up on blank walls or on the main floor by registration. To this, we once had a large "Welcome to the National Sports Forum banners hung by the hotel's main registration booth. Of course this jumbo welcome banner contained the logo of our hosting city. After the event, we presented this jumbo banner to the head of our host city's sports commission. He was thrilled, and what the heck was I going to do with it anyway?

But more than just banners, don't forget your sponsors with your on-site session signage. We always have stand alone foam-core easel signs created every year that are headed: "The NSF thanks its sponsors…" and then has the logos of our various sponsors printed below the header. Throughout the three-day event we simply move the signs around the hotel to insure people walking by are constantly seeing them.

- **On-Site Programs** – I've saved this one until almost the end because it deals with something we've not specifically addressed. We've walked around it a bit, but right here I want to hit it head on. And that is making sure that each of your sponsors has some stand-alone components in their package. I call these their "elements of exclusivity." Not to be confused with "category exclusivity" which we addressed previously.

But by elements of exclusivity, what I'm really getting at is making sure you include elements within each of your packages that allow each of your sponsors to stand alone by themselves.

With a lot of what we've covered above, program ads, banners, your website and the like, your sponsors are generally lumped together. To a certain extent that can be fine. However, what will really make your sponsorships sparkle is having a component or components within each of your sponsorship packages where the line shines solely and separately on each of your sponsors.

This is where dissecting your event can really come in handy. If your event includes a "welcome breakfast" or a "farewell banquet," have this presented by one of your sponsors. Coffee breaks should be "compliments of" one of your sponsors. A special panel discussion or one of your keynote speakers within the meeting can be "presented by" one of your sponsors.

I mentioned earlier that our room key cards feature one of our sponsors. Our biweekly e-zine is sponsored. We do a daily newsletter recapping all the events at the forum each day and it's "compliments of" one of our sponsors. Our main stage is named after one of our sponsors.

You're limited only by your creativity. Get crazy and have fun! But make sure that your sponsors are presented in a positive light and are woven throughout the entire event.

- **Intangible Assets** – We talked a lot about this earlier, so let me close by making sure that as you start jotting down the specific programs and elements that you'll be able to offer in each category, you make sure that you keep intangible benefits in mind.

  In the next chapter we're going to start talking about how to price your sponsorship packages. Keep in mind (as you start to move into this next section), that price has everything to do with "worth." In the final analysis, those intangible benefits are all-too-often worth far more than the tangible, quantifiable ones.

So that said, it's now time to close the file, at least for the time being, on your assets and on your property's sponsor-able components. We're going to come back and revisit these components in a couple chapters when we start getting into putting together your proposal packages. But for now, know that you're starting into the home stretch. You've laid a solid foundation and have only now to go over pricing before we go ahead and let you loose on the sponsorship world out there.

So, if you're ready, let's talk money…

Chapter Eight

"It's Not What It IS... It's What It's WORTH"

Affixing a "Dollars & Sense"
Price Tag to Your Property

This is actually going to be the first of two chapters here in the book where I get into a discussion on money. It's that important. After all, isn't that one of the main reasons you started down the sponsorship road in the first place?

In this chapter, I'm going to spend the next few pages talking about ways, via tips, strategies and insights, into helping you to figure out how to assign prices to your sponsorship packages. Later I'll devote a complete chapter to money and concentrating on the art of negotiation.

All that said, before you can start to negotiate a price, you have to begin by setting a price.

And, with that as the objective, I'm going to lead off this section by laying out three "true-isms" I've learned over the years about setting prices:

- *It's not about what it IS...it's about what it's WORTH!* (Admittedly I liked that one so much I decided to name the entire chapter after it!)

- *Learn how to sell money at a discount.*

- *Most people tend to under-value their 'assets' not over-value them.*

By taking each one of these statements separately and collectively, you'll come away with a pretty clear understanding of how I preach pricing. So let's break it down...

It's not about what it IS, it's about what it's WORTH!

Or more accurately, what it's worth to someone else. When it comes to pricing, truer words have never been spoken. Because in the end, nobody really cares about what you think your sponsorship is worth, they only care about what *they* think its worth. Price it too high and watch everyone quickly pass you by. Price it too low and you'll be spending the next year kicking yourself that you left way too much money on the table.

So the key to capturing both the sponsor's attention as well as their dollars is to do the best job you can to position your property as something that is truly worth a premium to be affiliated with. Simply stated, the better you can position your property, the more you can charge.

Selling Money at a Discount

You can dress this line up any way you want but in the end, that's really all you're doing here when it comes to selling your sponsorships.

Face it, chances are excellent that no one is going to agree to sponsor you or your property as a favor to you, or because they like you. Not that that couldn't happen, but it's not very likely. In reality, companies are ultimately going to agree to sponsor you for one reason and one reason only—because they believe it to be a good business decision.

Successful companies recognize that wise business decisions frequently start with good investments. There's an old adage that says: It takes money to make money, an old chestnut that is indeed the lynchpin of many a growing firm out there.

Recognizing this, decision makers are generally only too happy to put forth some seed money, but only if and when they're convinced that they'll get it back times two, times three, times ten dollars for every dollar they give up going in.

So, when considering your property, the shrewd business executive is primarily looking at your program as an investment. There's a cost to be borne, just as there is in buying traditional advertising, but it's an upfront cost that carries, hopefully, a backend return.

So your mission is to successfully convince contemplating decision-makers that in sponsoring your event, meeting, conference or boot camp, what they're doing, in reality, is buying money at a discount. For the price of a few dollars going in, you're going to give them access to an outstanding herd of interested consumers that will, when cultivated, return those dollars many times over coming back.

Most Under-Value, Not Over-Value

This last truism is something I've observed from years of looking at what people charge for access to their herd. This is especially true with those folks just starting out in selling sponsorship. Reason being, that we tend, as a society, to put a premium on what we don't have than on what we do have.

Think about yourself as a kid heading into Christmas. By the time December rolls around you're completely obsessed about that shiny new bike or video game you've had your eye on. It's the last thing you think about before you close your eyes at night, and the first thing you think about every morning. But invariably, two months, heck, in some cases two weeks, after you get it, it's lying out in the rain completely forgotten. (Not overly damaging for the bike, but pretty fatal for the video game!)

The same thing is true in buying and selling sponsorships years later as an adult. You've already got the herd; chances are you've had them for years. That's nothing particularly new or novel for you, but for an outside entity—someone wanting to reach the very people housed under your roof—what you represent is a tremendous opportunity for new business and incremental sales.

There's such a thing as being unrealistic, and you certainly don't want to blow yourself out of the water right out of the gate by pricing yourself unreasonably high in relation to what you're offering in return and/or what the market will bear. But there's also such a thing as giving your access away for a song.

Getting a Fair Price for a Fair Product

So how do you go about setting a fair price for a fair product?

There's several ways to do it. I personally prefer the old fashioned way, evaluate your herd going in and do your homework.

Evaluating your herd – For some property-owners, the value of their herd is in the sheer size of their numbers. Maybe you've got 5,000 members in your association or 20,000 subscribers to your monthly newsletter. All good stuff. Go with it.

But for many of us, we don't have a staggeringly large herd. Well, not yet anyway, but we're working on it!

And that's okay, too. But in cases such as that what you're going to want to promote is the quality of your herd not necessarily the quantity. You're going to want to drill down deeper in your research and sell your prospective sponsors on the characteristics and buying capabilities of your members/subscribers/attendees.

I mentioned one of my mentors, Dan Kennedy, earlier in this book, and one of his axioms is "The riches are in the niches!" That's true in just about every walk of business out there, especially in selling those smaller groups.

Remember back when I talked about researching out the spending commonalities of your herd? Great sums of money can often be generated from small groups of people, but only if you're able to reach those people.

In the example I used, I took a relatively small herd of 200 chiropractors that your research showed spent, on average, about $20K-$25K a year on printing to actively run and promote their business in a given year. That's not an unusually large group of people, and the sums they're spending on printing isn't an unwieldy amount of money. But when combined, this group in this exercise is spending $4.6 million each year on printing. That's a ton of money!

What printer out there wouldn't be interested in tapping into that group?

So don't fixate on the size of your herd, lamenting that they're not bigger, younger, smarter, or stronger. Absolutely grow your numbers, but while that's underway, dig to uncover those spending commonalities and go after the companies out there that can see the riches in your niches.

Do your homework – In many ways, selling a sponsorship is oftentimes not all that dissimilar than selling a house. A lot of what you'll be able to sell your house for depends on what the other houses in the neighborhood are selling for. That's the good news. The bad news is that it's invariably much easier to learn what the houses in your neighborhood are selling for than what other sponsorships are costing out at!

But that's also the good news too. Houses are commodities. If you don't like this one, I've got another one just down the street here to show you—and they're far more price agreeable!

You don't want to become "commoditized." Commodities are bought on price. You want to get bought on value. So while it definitely behooves you to find out what sort of ballpark other properties are going for, don't get overly hung up on what other people are charging for their event.

I don't have any vested interest in saying this, but one of the best places I've found to learn about what other groups charge for their sponsorships is IEG.

They put on a number of annual conferences, meetings, and webinars all pertaining to the various aspects of sponsorship and produce a monthly newsletter on the topic as well. I've taken part in a lot of it and have invariably found their products to be excellent— helpful, insightful and very educational.

Within their catalogue, IEG has a number of publications that discuss the pricing and packaging of sponsorships. You would be wise to check these out.

You'll quickly learn, as you study the topic of sponsorship pricing, that there's not some magic pricing formula out there. Back in the old days when I first went to work for the San Diego Padres, the formula for pricing our promotions at that time was to take the hard cost of the event or the promotional premiums we were giving away and charge the sponsor half of what it was costing us. Not having a lot of experience in the business, I remember asking my boss how we came to that formula? "I don't know," he replied, "that's the way we've always done it!"

So I started charging more for our sponsorships. Within a year I was basing my sponsorship fee on the full price of the events or premiums. And I got it. So I started charging more than the full price—got that too!

Along the way what I discovered is that a lot of it is just trial and error. Put it out there, run it up the flagpole and see who salutes.

Remember, the objective for you is the price. But the objective for the sponsor is the value of the access. As long as you can demonstrate to your prospective sponsor that in sponsoring you, they stand an excellent chance to double … triple … quadruple whatever they paid you as a sponsorship fee—you've got a deal!

But don't just "talk the talk." As we discussed right off the top in the beginning of this book, you've got to be able to actively and willingly "walk the walk." Once you sign that deal, it's got to become one of your primary responsibilities to partner with your sponsors in helping them to achieve a return on their investment. Remember, the real value to you isn't in the initial sale, it's in the resale. It's in all the renewals…year-after-year…from your many happy sponsors. You take good care of them and they'll take good care of you for many, many years to come.

As for precisely what you should charge, well, I don't have any "magic pricing formula" to offer to you here. But what I do have is some sound advice as you start to think about setting your sponsorship package prices.

- **Sell Your Assets** – As we covered earlier, you have two kinds of assets to your property, tangible assets and intangible assets.

It's technically possible to establish a set value on an event's tangible assets (i.e. the value of being featured on your ticket stock, on your event banners or on your website). There are organizations; IEG is one of them, which have established a rate card on what a tangible asset is worth.

But trust me, you're not going to be real happy with the prices they come up with. For instance, IEG says that the value of a company's name being on a banner is worth something like one-half of one cent per viewing. So if you were to have 200 people at your meeting and you "guesstimated" that each of these people walked by your sponsor logoed banners—looking at them, let's say 200 times each over a two-day period.

---

200 people x 200 viewings x $.005 per viewing = $200

Ouch! That's not a lot of money. I don't know about you, but I wouldn't be overly thrilled to be out there pulling in $200 checks for my sponsorships!

So know that the key is NOT in the tangible assets, but in the intangible ones! Sure you've got to have the tangible assets out there, every package requires them and every sponsor expects them.

But the real money is in the intangible assets or benefits you've got going for you. It's in the limited access you're giving to your prospective sponsors to have unencumbered access to your herd. It's in giving them the things they frankly couldn't buy elsewhere. You're not just selling them bodies. They could buy bodies anywhere. No, what you're selling them is high quality prospects, and you're doing it in a unique, imaginative and non-threatening way.

Five Pieces of Advice on Price

- Sell the SIZZLE ...Not the Steak - It's true in advertising and it's just as true in selling sponsorships! What you want to sell to your prospective sponsors are the benefits to be had by sponsoring your event, not the features.

Tangible assets are features. This many tickets, the "cost" of that trade show booth space, the full-page ad in your official program and so forth. Features are the kinds of benefits that are measurable, quantifiable and, invariably, not worth a whole lot.

But it's in the *intangible* assets where you'll find the benefits. And generally speaking, these are assets that can't be "traditionally measured." They're worth whatever you say they're worth because nobody else could go out there and buy it from someplace else.

For example, let's take "category exclusivity." When you offer up category exclusivity to a prospective sponsor what you're telling them is that no one else in that company's business category will be allowed to sponsor, exhibit, advertise ...or possibly even *attend* your event. Now that's a benefit! You're giving your prospective sponsor a completely clear field to reach your herd. No competition. That's worth something.

How much is that worth? I don't know—that would depend on your event, the size of your audience, the frequency of their exposure (in other words, how many times does your audience get together and for how long each time), the buying potential of those in attendance, and the competitiveness of the category.

In the sports world, for instance, category exclusivity is a highly desirable intangible benefit in such categories as soft drinks, automotive, and beer. For each, the sports fan in attendance is a prime consumer of these products. And with each, there's a lot of competition in each category.

The result is that category exclusivity is really worth a lot to each of these players in the category. Such would not be true in the sports world, in the category of medical instruments or the daily newspaper.

Most cities only have one major daily these days, so there's not going to be a lot of competition in that category. Not a lot of value to the daily news to want to lock their competition out.

- **Do Your Homework** - Look around, who else out in your community is putting on meetings that have sponsors? Look in your local commercial newspaper in the business section. Or better yet, if you have a business daily or weekly in your area, check in there for upcoming conferences, meetings and seminars.

Ideally you'll be able to locate a group, association, or meeting that is in your niche neighborhood that's coming to town. (You probably won't find a whole lot of input and cooperation from others who are putting on gatherings in your exact niche, but close, complimenting groups that put on meetings can be a real gold mine for you.)

Reach out and contact the organizers of some of these other meetings. They don't have to be local meetings, but it helps. I have a couple of conference organizers that I openly share numbers with that live on the other side of the country. But in all of these instances, our relationships started with our meeting one another in person. I've found that meeting face-to-face with another organizer warms both of you up more to the interests of openly sharing information.

Maybe you don't have any sponsorship nuggets to share with these other organizers, that's okay. They might benefit by gaining your insights on some affordable meeting space in your community or learning from you who some of the local printers are in your town that do a great job for a reasonable price.

You, on the other hand, want to pick their brains about their sponsors and advertisers.

While we're on this topic, let me also advise that you should start getting into the practice of attending other meetings, preferably those that have sponsors attached to them. The topic doesn't even have to be remotely connected to what you're offering. In fact, you'll oftentimes find more value out of taking part in a completely unrelated meeting or gathering.

Why?

Simple: there's a certain amount of "in-breeding" that you start to find when you circulate only within other meetings inside your discipline. Sure, everyone shops the competition—that's a wise thing to do. But it also tends to create a certain sense of "same-ness" to all the meetings out there in your industry. The same layout, the same speakers, or types of speakers, the same exhibitors, stage layout... even food.

Break out of the mold. See how other organizers put on their meetings, their breakout sessions, how they layout their trade show halls, and how they recognize and promote their sponsors and advertisers. Do this and I guarantee you you'll learn a ton.

When you're at these other meetings wait for a nice break in the organizer's flow to approach them. Generally speaking, as the meeting starts to wind down on the last day, that's a good time to approach the organizer, introduce yourself, and ask for their card. Tell them who you are and what you do. And ask them if it's okay once the dust settles if you could give them a call and talk a little shop with them?

Then, once their meeting is over, give them a few days to decompress, but not too much time where they forget about your introduction, and give them a call. For me, I give them about a week, then I follow-up.

Compliment them on what you really liked or learned about their event. Be genuine and sincere. Remind them again as to what it is you do, what your group make-up is, and then head to the point of your call. Thank them for their time and tell them that you're calling because you'd really appreciate being able to ask them some questions about their sponsorship packages.

Not that you're asking them to reveal any proprietary information, but you'd like to ask them about how they find their sponsors? How long have they had sponsors attached to their meetings? What kinds of sponsors do they look for and what kinds of sponsorship packages do they offer up to their meetings or association gatherings?

And as you start to get warmed up, don't forget that turn-about is fair play. Ask them if there's any information you can lend them about what you do with your group? It's important you offer to give as well as get information with your fellow organizer. What you're endeavoring to do here is to put this other person at ease, to alleviate any edge or suspicions they might have as to who you are or what it is you want.

Once they recognize that you're not a threat, you'll generally find them to be more forthcoming in answering your questions. In some cases their organization might have a sponsorship overview or other written documentation as to what they offer, and what they charge, that they might send you. That's great, go with the flow.

Or go in the other direction and come away from the other organizer's meeting or boot camp with a roster of who their sponsors are. Better yet, when you're at that meeting or conference, seek out representatives from those sponsoring companies and meet them.

Oftentimes a benefit of being a sponsor is that representatives of the sponsoring company/companies are invited to sit on panels or lead breakout sessions. Gives you a perfect opportunity to go up to them afterwards, introduce yourself and get their business card.

WARNING: Sponsors of meetings can sometimes be a bit gun shy after a presentation as they're used to getting hit up by attendees wanting their company's money or business. Knowing this, the key for you is to disarm the sponsor by assuring them that the only thing you want from them is their insights on their sponsorship experience.

Tell them about your group and that you're just getting your sponsorships off the ground. That said, ask them if it would be okay for you to contact them by phone in the next week in order to ask them some questions about what their company sponsors, what elements they like to see in their sponsorship packages, how they activate their sponsorships and what different sponsorships should cost.

Admittedly, some of these folks might big league you implying they're much too busy, much too important, to trifle with you. Fine, perhaps they could steer you to one of their assistants in their organization that might have a few minutes for you?

In the end, keep your eye on the prize. What you're looking to start building is a network of contacts who can help you to gain as many insights as you can into what sponsorships cost and what they look like in your area. You'll start to see interesting components start to surface, interesting benefits that other meetings are offering up to their sponsors/advertisers and what these things cost.

You're going to find this information to be highly valuable to you as you start to put pencil to paper on your packages. The more homework you do, the more comfortable you're going to become as you start to fine-tune and finalize your packages.

- **Practice Price Elasticity** - Coming right out of the chute, as you'll probably be if you're just starting to offer up sponsorships to your gatherings, you're apt to seriously under-price your packages. That's fine—it's not the end of the world.

Just because you're cheap now doesn't mean you have to *stay* cheap. Every event starts somewhere, and truth be told, if you're just starting out in offering up sponsorship affiliations, why not feature your "bottom floor pricing" as one of the genuine benefits prospective sponsors are going to want to jump on by getting involved with your organization right now?

As a sponsorship salesperson, one of the most important sponsorships you'll ever sell to your event is your first one.

For one thing, it'll validate within your own mind that what you have is of interest to other companies out there. What you have is worth something to an outside entity. That's excellent!

But better than that, one sponsorship quickly leads to another. And another. And before you know it, you'll have a nice healthy mix of affiliated companies—all highly interested in your herd and all looking forward to you doing your magic.

Which is all wonderful, but keep in mind however that as your property/ association/meeting size/customer base continues to grow, so too with it grows the value of what you're offering to your sponsors. The more you give them, the more access, the more exposure, the more involvement, plus the larger your herd, the more you can command in return for the access you're giving to these sponsors.

Once you're off and running, don't be afraid to raise your prices. And don't get caught up in that "Well, it doesn't really cost me that much to offer this" mentality. Who cares what it costs you; it's what its worth to your sponsors.

We raise our prices just about every year at the Sports Forum. But hand-in-glove with this is that we do our utmost to make sure that our sponsors always feel that we're thinking about them and trying to help them gain market share out in the sports world.

Does that mean we never run into price resistance? Sure we do. Let's face it — nobody likes to pay more money. But I'd like to think we do a pretty good ongoing job of demonstrating the value of being a sponsor of the Sports Forum. Sure, we've lost sponsors over the many years, but it's not because they didn't feel they got value from their association with our group.

We'll get more into price resistance once we start talking about negotiation in the next section; however, for now, it's important that you begin to get comfortable with establishing your sponsorship benefits and your sponsorship pricing.

As we wrap up "Aim!" you know exactly what it is you're selling to prospective sponsors, you've gained some tips as to where to go to find them, you now know how to put your sponsorship packages together and, lastly, you've gained some wisdom as to how to set your prices for your sponsorship packages. In short, you're ready to go to market!

To you, sponsors represent two things. First, sponsors represent revenues in your pockets. And more than that, depending on how you structure your deals, sponsors can represent not just cash, but cash flow.

Which can be incredibly important when you're just getting your group, meeting, or association started. Or perhaps you're already established, but you are thinking about expanding? A second or third meeting in a different part of the country? Or maybe a similar event, but targeted to a different audience? Expansion requires capital, and at times like these, sponsorship revenues coming to you periodically throughout the year can be extremely important to you in operating your business.

But in addition to revenues, sponsorships deliver a second value—a hidden benefit if you will. Sponsors bring with them a certain cache that in and of itself will help you to promote your event, group, or association. And that can be even more valuable to you!

There's another old adage that you're known by the company you keep, and that works both ways with sponsors. The sponsors are paying for the privilege of being associated with your organization, and at the same time, their affiliation with your group tells would-be attendees or members a lot about your significance.

- **The Power of the Association** - There have been times over the years in putting on the Sports Forum that I have agreed to accept less money from certain sponsors because I recognized how important having their name associated with my event would be out in my market. The message to your prospects of having Corporation "XYZ" as a sponsor of yours is significant—and should definitely not be overlooked.

And not just with your potential attendees, but with other sponsors as well. Trust me, the other companies out there will look real hard at the other companies that are sponsoring your group, meeting, or association.

Final note on the power of association: Success breeds success, and as your event grows in size and reputation, you'll find that you won't need to discount your sponsorship fees to attract name sponsors to your gatherings. "It is what it is" will become your new mantra. But when you're just getting your event or sponsorship component off the ground, be open to doing what you have to do to get those first couple of big names to your sponsorship roster.

Chapter Nine

"It's Not WHAT You Say..."

It's HOW You Say It...

After giving this some thought, I decided to title this chapter in honor of something my wife used to say to my oldest son once upon a time back when he was five years old. (He's in grad school now, so this was a l-o-n-g time ago!)

But it was so logical then and it taught both my son and his dad a valuable lesson in the "Art of Sales and Effective Human Interaction."

Back when Alex was four years old or so, he was like most every other young master out there and pretty skilled at going after what he wanted. In the process, he failed to understand that there was more than one side to every equation (namely, his). And if he didn't agree with your decision as to what it was he wanted: Phew—he'd let you know about it!

In short, he wanted what he wanted. And nothing less would be tolerated.

That approach to life didn't work too well when he was five years old, and, as we've all come to learn, it doesn't work a whole lot better when we're 45 years old either.

Fortunately, under the patient guidance of my wife, my son eventually came to learn that he could open up a lot more doors a lot easier if he went after it with a good attitude, a pleasant approach, flexibility and with consideration for what others wanted in pursuit of what he was after.

And along the way, in so doing, he learned that oftentimes it wasn't so much what he said... it was in how he said it that got the job done.

What a great lesson to learn early in life! And certainly something for us to keep in mind as we pursue securing sponsors for our own purposes.

More specifically, you now recognize that your ability to get what you want (sponsorship dollars) is going to be in large part predicated by your ability to give others (sponsors) what it is that they want (a.k.a: access to your "herd").

Do that and you're on your way.

However, a word to the wise. As you start gearing up for your sponsorship chase, you're not going to get a whole lot of time to make your pitch to your prospective sponsors. Sponsorship decision-makers are all too often busy, over-burdened, often harried executives who invariably won't stand still long enough in one place to allow you all the time you'd like to convince them how they can't live without sponsoring your group, meeting or association.

The Three Keys to Stating Your Case

In fact, what you're going to find is that it's oftentimes not always "how you say it" as it is "how quickly you can say it" and "how effectively you can make your case."

You need to be fully prepared going in and be armed with the necessary materials. Once in the door, you'll need to state your case quickly and convincingly. And know that more than likely you'll need to do this first on paper as chances are you won't get a face-to-face meeting unless, and until, you can convince the prospect that you represent a potential solution to their problems.

But, either way, on paper or done in-person, once you've described your event and stated the benefit to be had by the sponsor in underwriting your property, you then need to solicit and answer any of their questions or concerns. Completing that, it's time to close the deal.

It's not EASY, but Fortunately ...It IS Simple!

Easy? No, but it is simple!

There's a very simple process you need to follow in pursuing your sponsors. In cases where you are going in "cold" (in other words, going after a prospect you don't know or have never met before), you start with an "introductory letter," move into a "proposal" and finish with a "contract." That's your A-to-Z, and I'll cover them all.

So let's get started with the introductory letter.

Chapter Ten

"Getting to KNOW You..."

The Art of Getting Your Foot in the Door!

I f you've gotten this far, congratulations—you've now successfully completed your "sponsorship foundation."

In reaching this point, you've dissected your property, and, in the process created and developed an interchangeable roster of benefits you can now use in various combinations to create your sponsorship packages.

It's these benefits that will comprise all of the things you can do and access you can create for your sponsors that will, in turn, help them to accomplish their objectives.

And, as an event, meeting, or conference organizer, you now have a really good picture of not only what you have to sell, but who your market is, how many you "touch" and how you can take all those benefits you've put together to help your sponsors to meet their goals.

And finally, in addition to all of the above, you've done your homework and fashioned together a healthy roster of prospective companies you can now be going after. In doing so, you've uncovered objectives from each company that would well benefit from sponsoring your property. What remains now is taking it to the streets.

The Importance of a Great First Impression

You're now ready to start putting together your calling cards: your introductory letter and your follow-up sponsorship proposal.

We're going to take a good long look at the proposal later, but let's start the process by talking about the elements of a strong introductory letter.

NOTE: I'm personally a big fan of engaging in a three-step process when it comes to soliciting a prospective sponsor, especially if it's someone I've never met before. I've found I'm too easy to disregard or dismiss if I bundle a cold intro letter together with a proposal. I'd much rather try to pique their interest. Get on their radar screen, and then follow my introduction up with a follow-up phone call. Then, once the connection is made, send them a specific proposal. It's admittedly a longer process, but, in the end, my success ratio, if I've done my homework right, tends to be much higher.

The purpose of the introductory letter ... as its name implies, is to get you introduced. However, there's actually a second purpose of your Introductory Letter—the second purpose being to let the reader know that you'll be following up with a phone call. That's it.

It should be short, to the point, and it should definitely grab the reader's interest.

You can get 'em or lose 'em right there in the opening paragraph.

One of the best ways I've had success in getting my target's attention is to grab them with an opening that not only shows the reader I know something about their business, but, in the process, touches on an exposed nerve or a viable need I think they might have.

And one of the best ways you'll be able to do this is to draw down on the research you did on your prospect back in the "research phase." (If you skipped ahead, the research phase was the boning up you did on the industry back in the "Aim!" section.)

There must have been something about this prospect that flagged your attention when you were doing all your Internet research or periodical reading.

What was it that caused you to think this company might have an interest in reaching your members?

- Perhaps it was something in the industry trades that talked about how this prospect's company was looking to expand their market share into the specific market you star in?

- Or how the new technology they're rolling out is ideally suited for the market you serve?

- Perhaps you noticed a story in The Wall Street Journal that talked about the companies in your prospect's category and how they're all seemingly looking to attract the types of people that populate your boot camps?

- Or maybe it's something a key client of theirs mentioned to you at a cocktail party when he/she, upon learning about what you do, recommended that you reach out to their contact at "Company XYZ" and introduce yourself.

Whatever it was, there should be a clear-cut reason stated in the opening paragraph that explains why it is that you have taken the time to single them out to approach, and why they should have an interest and take the time to field your follow-up phone call.

And please, whatever you do, no generic "Dear Sir" letters. You're better than that. If you don't have a real tangible reason for writing to this company, save yourself a stamp and them a headache. They'll sniff you out in five seconds and your letter will hit the trash in less time than it took you to read this paragraph.

Taking Apart the "A-to-Z" of an Effective Introductory Letter

You need to tell them exactly what it was that brought you to them and how you can help them to solve their problems. To better illustrate... take a look at this hypothetical example here...

Date

Name
Title
Address
City, State, Zip

Dear (Person's Name),

I hope you won't mind my writing to you completely "... out of the blue" like this, but I just finished an article that ran in last week's "Sports Business News" about (company name's) new product launch with the New York Mets. I found this to be very interesting and I wanted to wish you good luck with this!

I also wanted to reach out and run something by you...

Your "widget," I believe, will prove to be a very beneficial product to the Mets, and something I suspect that will soon have you thinking about rolling out this out to all the other teams out there. If so – I truly believe my company can be of help to you.

Admittedly, I don't know everything about (company name's) business, but if there's one thing I've learned in my twenty-five years in the sports industry, it's that it's not enough to be the first one to market with a great product (which I think you definitely have), you have to be the first one to successfully roll it out across the market and do so affordably.

This is where I think we can be of help...

Get the idea? Let your prospect know right up front that you have a real purpose, a legitimate reason, for reaching out to them. Illustrate to them that you're familiar with what they're doing and that you're in a position to be of help to them.

---

*My company, **Seaver Marketing Group,** puts on **The National Sports Forum,** the largest cross-team marketing, sponsorship, advertising, sales and fan entertainment conference in North America. What makes the Forum so unique is that it's the only conference out there today that brings together a thoroughly diverse cross-section of the top marketing, sponsorship and sales executives from both the teams as well as league offices of the NFL, Major League Baseball, NBA, Major League Soccer and NHL.*

Our "core" is joined by many of their counter-parts from the Minor League teams, colleges, auto racing, horse racing and major sports associations. (Collectively ... our audience represents about as close to a "United Nations" of team/event sports as you're going to find under one roof.)

So what does this have to do with you... (you're probably wondering)?

_____

Notice that it's not until the sixth paragraph that I tell my prospect who I am? Admittedly, they're pretty short paragraphs, but that's not an accident—that's by design.

My fragile ego not withstanding, I know that nobody cares who I am until I give them a reason to! They only care about who they are and what they want! The strategy I'm using here admittedly flies in the face of conventional logic. Most folks, right from the get-go, would want to jump right in with the "here's who I am, and this is what I want" kind of language. Something like:

_____

Dear Mr. Smith,

My name is Ron Seaver and I'm the president of The National Sports Forum. I'm writing you today on behalf of the Sports Forum because I believe that your company would really benefit by exposure to our audience...

_____

Ugh—I've probably lost Mr. Smith by end of the first line! In his mind, he's translated my intro into:

Dear Mr. Smith,

My name is "some guy" and I'm with "who cares." And my company wants your money.... blah-blah-blah." (Followed by the sound of letter being crumpled and hitting the trash...)

I don't know about you, but I don't want to give Mr. Smith an excuse right out of the gate to recycle my efforts. So what I would advise you to do instead is to come up with something that will do a better job of grabbing his/her attention. And *then* say who you are.

From there, notice in my second section above that, because I don't think Mr. Smith will be readily familiar with my property, I go into a little bit of depth about what The National Sports Forum is? Not just what it is, but what makes it unique. We're certainly not the only sports conference going on out there, so I need to establish, right off the bat, what distinguishes our conference from all the other conventions and meetings going on out there.

And then, having done that, it's now time to tie the opening section together with the second section by getting inside his head and saying what I envision he is saying as he reads my letter, "Okay, so why are you writing to me?"

There's an axiom in our industry that isn't all that unusual from what exists in a number of other tight-knit industries out there. And it says that it's not WHAT you know... it's WHO you know.

And while that may be true elsewhere, nowhere is it MORE true than in the sports team industry. Ours is a very small and connected "niche" – in many ways, likened to a "fraternity" or a bonded social organization.

What you're going to find (...as you begin your efforts in trying to navigate through the professional sports industry...), is that it's senior decision-makers are inordinately difficult to get a hold of and once you do – can be equally as difficult to get focused on your product.

Phone calls don't get returned, e-mails get ignored ... and direct mail solicitations go unanswered.

What you'd really like to do is get a face-to-face meeting, but even if you could, short of spending a small fortune flying around the country, how can you make this happen?

That's where the Sports Forum comes in...

Introductions concluded, I'm now getting down to business. Mr. Smith here has a product and a good one at that. But he's also got a problem. He may not even realize it yet, so why don't I help him? For his product to have success, he's going to have to reach out to a decidedly difficult to isolate group of customers. They're busy, they're scattered, focused on other things—they're tough to pin down.

I want to focus on that problem, accentuate that pain, and then offer Mr. Smith up a solution, most notably, *my* solution...

For a company like (company name), with an interest in potentially tying their product into a number of high profile sports organizations, the NSF serves as the perfect "one stop shopping" place for you to not only meet literally dozens of the top team/ league marketing and sales "decision-makers", but to let the entire industry know WHO you are and WHY they should want to do business with you.

Now it's time to head for the close...

In (#) quick months we'll be getting the industry together in (location). And that being the case, I thought now would be an excellent time to reach out, introduce myself, and tell you how I think we can help (company name) use our event to best position yourselves to literally hundreds of the "key decision-makers" that you're going to be looking to reach in the coming months.

To that interest, I'd like to give you a call next week and follow up on this. I think once I have a chance to learn more from you first-hand about your team marketing initiatives, I can be more specific in outlining opportunities to you that will help (company name) gain the access and presence you're looking for as you take your "widget" to the next level.

Thanks very much (Person's Name). I'll look forward to speaking with you next week.

Sincerely yours,
THE NATIONAL SPORTS FORUM
Ron Seaver
President

P.S. I hope you won't mind but I've taken the liberty of enclosing a couple pieces of "propaganda" on The National Sports Forum (herein). I think they'll prove helpful to you in illustrating not only the types of topics we cover at the Forum (...of which I think your product would be a great fit...), but of the kinds of senior-level speakers that are all a part of each year's event as well.

P.P.S. If exposing your product to the industry's decision-makers is important to you – I can't think of a better place for you to do this than at the Forum. That said, I'll look forward to speaking with you next week!

You end your introductory letter by identifying for them, in a general manner, how your solution can help them solve one of their distinguishing problems. And then you tell that you will be back in touch and when you'll be back in touch, with them to discuss this more specifically.

And lastly, don't forget a P.S. or two. Repeated studies have shown that the P.S. is invariably one of the most widely read pieces of your entire document. It's the lasting impression you'll leave them with—and it sums up for them exactly what's in it for them.

Granted what I've sketched out above is a completely cold introductory cover letter. Ideally you'd be better off if there was a common acquaintance who could introduce you to the prospect you're trying to reach, but many times you don't always get that luxury and you have to go in alone.

Having said that, chances are if your industry does indeed intersect with the company you're targeting—there's someone in your world who might also know either the person you're trying to contact, or another person in his/her department. In the real world, for example, I would've started my efforts in the example above by reaching out to one of my buddies at the New York Mets. I would've asked them to coordinate an introduction with the prospect I was trying to reach.

But you won't always have the benefit of a mutual contact. In those cases, I've admittedly had some pretty good success just using a cold introductory letter similar to the one I've drafted above.

Bottom line, when you're coming in cold, or even lukewarm, the key is to get your prospect's attention, tell them who you are, what you do, and why it is that you think you can be of service to them.

Then either ask them to take an action, or tell them what action you're going to take and close with one or two P.S.'s.

You're now ready for step two—the follow-up call.

Chapter Eleven

"Listen 'n Learn"

Follow Up Calls & Sales Meetings

In all my years of putting on the Sports Forum, I've had the good fortune of getting to meet a number of our industry's smartest, most innovative sports leaders out there. Commissioners, team owners, network heads...you name it. But one of the most impressive leaders I've ever gotten to know is a gentleman by the name of Jon Spoelstra. Jon is ... in addition to being a best selling author, a teacher and the former president of a number of professional teams and sports organizations.

The Three Things You MUST Do on Your First Sponsorship Sales Call

Jon is widely recognized in our industry as one of the brightest, most innovative leaders in all of professional sports, particularly in the fields of sales and marketing where he's unparalleled. And one of the things I've learned from Jon is that there's a real art to the follow-up call or initial sales meeting. And no one does this better than he does. Simply stated, Jon teaches his sales team to sit down, shut up, and learn something.

Because most of Jon's prospects tend to live in the same area as one of his Major or Minor League franchises, he's able to skip the follow-up call step and go straight to asking for a face-to-face meeting. (If you live in the same area as your sponsorships prospects, you too should close your introductory letters by saying that you'll give your prospect a call the following week to hopefully set up a convenient time for you to stop in and get a chance to meet them face-to-face).

For us at the Sports Forum, none of our sponsor prospects live anywhere near where we do, so we generally have to go with our follow-ups over the phone. Which is fine because Jon's rules apply whether you're doing it eyeball-to-eyeball or voice to ear.

Why Your First Objective Is Not to Sell Your Prospect ANYTHING!

The key to success in your initial follow-up has little to do with your mouth — and almost everything to do with your ears!

Which is apt to be difficult for many, if not most, salespeople. Sales folks generally tend to think that their job is to talk and do their utmost to convince the person on the other side of the table or phone that they have what this person needs. They're wrong. It's the salesperson's primary job to sell. And they can sell by helping their prospect to solve his or her problems or needs. But how can you do that if you don't know what those problems are?

Simple: you can't. You need to first know what the other person is looking to do before you can help them to do it. So Jon's first rule to the teams he consults with is to take all their boilerplate sales proposals and generic sales materials and throw them out the window! In fact, when one of Jon's sales associates goes on a sales call the only things they're allowed to bring with them are a baseball cap from their team, a notepad, and a pen.

Their instructions are simple: Give the baseball cap to the prospect and bring the notepad back full of notes from your potential sponsor. If you do the same thing—and I suggest you do—your job right now is not to sell the prospect anything. Nothing! Even if you think you know the perfect thing for them going in, hold it in check!

The Five Answers You Should Come Away with on That First Sales Call

Your only task right now is to fill up your notepad with valuable input from the sponsor-prospect you're meeting with or talking to on the phone. And the way you're going to get all that valuable input for your notepad is to ask your prospect many insightful information-seeking questions about:

- Their business

- Their product

- What it does

- Who buys it

- What they're wanting to accomplish

You get answers to those five questions—and given what those answers are—I defy you to not sell something to these prospects!

As Jon would tell you, if you are patient, ask the right questions and listen intently to what they have to say in response, your sales prospect will basically tell you everything you need to know to make them a sale.

It's that's simple. Notice again, I didn't say easy. It's not easy, but it is simple!

And please, don't be one of those phony insincere sales turkeys, the kind who asks a question only so they can launch into an explanation of what *they think* you need. The kind that doesn't let the prospect fully explain their position or their thoughts before jumping in with "well, we have this great product that does..." (The loud explosion you just heard is the sound of the sales turkey shooting himself squarely in the foot!)

Instead, what you need to do is systematically go down this roster of five questions based on the points above, ask them and take copious informative notes when they respond. Obviously some of your prospects' answers will lend themselves to additional follow-up questions, which is fine. In fact, it's great! Ask away. This'll all prove to be very informative for you, and, frankly, most business executives love to talk about their businesses!

(In fact, the more they talk, the brighter they tend to think you are! Not a bad thing!)

When you're finished, kindly thank the prospect for their time and insights. Tell them that they've given you a lot of good things that you can now work on and with it some great ideas as to how your company can be of assistance in helping them to hit their objectives. If you're there in person, stand up, shake their hand and leave. Before you go, ask them if they have any sales collateral about their company that you could take back with you as well. On the phone, bring a polite end to the conversation after making sure you have all the relevant website addresses and any other information the prospect offers. You're now ready to go back to work and get started on creating your masterpiece - your sponsorship proposal.

Chapter Twelve

"But WAIT – There's MORE!"

The Art of Writing Effective Sponsorship Proposals

Now that you know precisely what you have to offer and exactly what your prospect wants to accomplish—it's simply going to be a matter of your now marrying up the two.

Back in section two you created a running roster of all of the sponsor-able components of your boot camps, meetings, association gatherings and seminars. Each of those components lends themselves to accomplishing different things for your sponsor.

For instance, if a potential sponsor is looking for visibility and name recognition with your herd, then things such as getting their name/logo out in front of people via stage banners, signage, ticket stock, and program ads are going to be of interest to them.

If, however, what would best benefit your sponsor is to give your attendees a chance to use or sample their products, then improvise accordingly. Include in your sponsorship proposal the opportunity to have samples of the sponsor's product placed in the attendee's registration kit and/or have staff set up at the main hall entrance/exit handing out samples of the sponsor's product to people as they come in.

Perhaps you have a sponsor who wants to meet some very specific people within your herd? Not a problem, simply create a special invitation-only reception or private cocktail party that is hosted by your sponsor with invitations sent out to carefully selected individuals in advance of the conference.

The key here is to carefully cull through all the notes you've taken paying particular attention to what it was the prospect told you they're wanting to accomplish. If you're unsure, don't be afraid to contact them again and ask them. Also, given you put on meetings, it would be wise during your initial sit-down or follow-up phone call, to ask them if their company currently participates or sponsors any industry meetings or conventions. If yes, which meetings do they go to or sponsor? What do they like about their involvement with these other shows? What do they dislike about these other shows?

The Three Steps to Combining What You Have ...with What They Want

The more information you possess, the more powerful and effective your response will be.

Here's how I break the proposal down in steps:

- *Step One:* **Information gathering** - Check. You've returned from your meeting or finished your phone call and now have a ton of very specific information about what your prospect's goals are: who their core audience is (i.e. who they're looking to sell to), what they're wanting to say to these people, what their product/service does (i.e. features and benefits) and, lastly, what they're wanting to accomplish sales and/or marketing-wise.

- *Step Two:* **Marrying what you have to offer with what they're looking to accomplish** - Check again. As we talked about in the opening of this chapter, you came back from your meeting with your wheels spinning.

 You've carefully reviewed their objectives against what the different components are that your meeting/association has to offer. Each of your "components" accomplishes different things, so select those components that best match up to the needs, wants, and desires of your prospective sponsor.

- *Step Three:* **Put it down on paper** - This will be your proposal, the coming together of needs and solutions.

As you set to the task of drafting your proposal, keep in mind you don't need to write *War and Peace.* That's a mistake I see way too many sponsorship sales people do, and it's unbelievably counterproductive!

As I mentioned in the "Ready" section, the people you're dealing with—be they small business owner, restaurant manager, agency vice president or Fortune 500 brand manager—they're all busy multi-tasking types of people. They haven't got enough time to sit down and eat lunch, let alone wade through a 75-page dissertation about your wonderful event and the history of your organization! It seems obvious, yet you'd be amazed at how many top name organizations make this cardinal mistake. It's almost as if they believe that the heavier their proposal is, the better its chance for success! Well, it's not. As proposals go, they make better doorstops than they do sales vehicles!

Instead you should shoot for a maximum of four pages. As part of the Sports Forum, we've been interviewing 50 of the top corporate sports sponsors and advertisers in the United States every two years since 1995, and they tell us the same thing: "I don't need to know how many titles you've won, or what your exciting new scoreboard looks like. What I want to know is: what have you got, what do I get, and how much does it cost?"

So go with those basics and break your proposal out into the following sections.

Section One: The Opening – There's a very real chance that the person you met with isn't going to be the only one to review your proposal, you should start with a small brief introduction that references your initial meeting and reminds the reader about what your event is and why it's a good match.

Section Two: Their Goals/Objectives – Again, you're encapsulating this from the information you took back from you initial meeting/phone call. Go through your list of goals and select the three or four goals they gave you that match up closest with the ingredients that exist in the benefits in your sponsorship package.

Section Three: Your Sponsorship Package – Here's where you break out each one of your sponsorship package "ingredients," explaining what they are, what's in them and how this ingredient helps them to accomplish one (or more...) of the aforementioned goals from section two.

Section Four: The Bottom Line – It's money time. Here is where you tell them how much the laid out sponsorship package is going to cost them—making sure to lay out the payment deadlines as well.

Section Five: Next Step – Tell them what they should do next, and finally...

Section Six: The Close – Sum it all up. Reinforce how you have carefully and selectively taken their goals and created tie-in components within your "product" that enables them to specifically meet those stated objectives. With that you close by thanking them for their time and consideration and let them know that you will be following up on this shortly to answer any questions or address any concerns they might have. Sincerely yours…and you're out of there.

"Short 'n' Sweet" – and Other Quick Hitters

That's all there is to it, folks. Nothing long-winded, cumbersome or vague about it. Before I close this section, let me give you a couple "quick-hitters" or tips on crafting an effective, attractive proposal:

- *Short 'n' Sweet* – As we talked about in the opening, keep your proposal to 3-4 pages.

- *Use Bullet Points* – A lot of people tend to "scan" first and get the gist of what you've got to say before they wade in. They love to see things condensed into bullet points. If you can concentrate and consolidate your points, so much the better.

- *Headlines* – Copywriting experts talk a lot about the "dual readership path." This references what I was just talking about. People tend to scan a document first looking for the salient points that jump out at them. They'll "read" your proposal once concentrating on bullet points, pictures, captions and headlines. That kind of gives them a "road map" of where this proposal is going.

Sponsorship people also tend to want to start at the back and read forward. In other words, they want to know: *"How much is this gonna cost me?"* before they decide how much stock they want to put in what you're saying. We'll talk in depth about pricing and negotiating coming up, but, for now, make sure to break up your sections with bold headlines that clearly separate one piece from the other.

What you really want to get away from are proposals that look like one gigantic "wall of type." If it looks like your proposal is going to be work to read, chances are excellent they won't read it! So break it up.

Pictures - Pictures are a great way to help make your proposal easier on the reader's eyes. Not that this has to be a "photo album," but an occasional shot of all your association members sitting in a general session or earnestly talking to one another doing business is a nice way to get your point across attractively. Remember, a picture says a thousand words. Take advantage of that.

Nice 'n' Clean - Once you're done, go back over it one last time for "eye-appeal."

And before you tuck that proposal in an envelope, ask yourself, "Does this proposal sell beer?" In other words, does your proposal clearly accomplish the prospect's stated objectives?" If it does, great, bombs away. If it doesn't, keep working.

SAMPLE SPONSORSHIP PROPOSAL

NATIONAL SPORTS FORUM™

February 7, 20XX
Name
President
Company
Street
City, State Zip

SPONSORSHIP PROPOSAL TO:
(COMPANY NAME) as Presenting Sponsor of
The 20XX-20XX NSF "Brought to You By..." Panel

Dear Name,

On behalf of our entire staff here at the National Sports Forum ("NSF"), we appreciate your allowing us this opportunity to present to (COMPANY NAME) the below-outlined 20XX-20XX NSF Sponsorship Package built around the National Sports Forum's "Brought to You By..." Panel.
In creating the sponsorship package that follows, we've made every effort to build in and incorporate elements that would accomplish the objectives you and I discussed on the phone.
More specifically, the sponsorship program that follows was designed to accomplish the following objectives for (COMPANY NAME):

   □ *Raise...and keep... (COMPANY NAME)'s name in the forefront of the minds of our patrons for the twelve months surrounding each NSF conference over the next three years.*

▫ *Become another "tool" in (COMPANY NAME)'s on-going industry awareness arsenal.*

▫ *Use the NSF as a platform from which to expose new (COMPANY NAME) products/services.*

▫ *Utilize all facets of the NSF to help cement (COMPANY NAME) as experts in our industry.*

▫ *Let the NSF help (COMPANY NAME) coordinate and serve as a conduit to facilitate new business introductions.*

That said, what follows is a "thumbnail" description of the "Brought to You By..." sponsorship program and a description of the components in your package designed to accomplish these objectives.

History of the "Brought to You By..." Super Panel: *The "Brought to You By..." Sponsor's Panel discussion is one of the Forum's signature events and has become a perennial favorite of our Forum attendees. Introduced in 20XX, this panel discussion is made up of individually selected corporate decision-makers who share their experience and expertise with our audience—a group comprised primarily of senior-level team, event and industry executives.*

As the sponsor of this panel, (COMPANY NAME) will have the spotlight all to yourself as you address our entire audi-ence...giving (COMPANY NAME) the opportunity to intro-duce the panel and present (COMPANY NAME)'s position, your products, services and technology, and how (COMPANY

NAME) enjoys its role as a vital member of the sports fraternity.

In addition, as sponsor of the "Brought to You By..." panel, (COMPANY NAME) is entitled to participate in the selection process of the panel invitees, providing (COMPANY NAME) with a perfect opportunity to bring in some corporate allies and partners.

Each year, we take great pride in organizing a panel that is composed of some of the most powerful sponsors in our industry, and having (COMPANY NAME) to help us add credence to what we're doing can only help us in continuing this effort. To date we have been able to include industry executives representing Anheuser-Busch, MasterCard International, Nextel, Gatorade, Siemens Canada, Coca-Cola, Visa USA, and McDonald's Corporation.

For 20XX: This coming year the Forum heads to Memphis, Tenn., with the "Brought to You By" Sponsor's Panel slated to run that Monday, January 28, 20XX. Because of its popularity, the panel discussion serves as the highlight of Monday afternoon with no competing events scheduled to occur at the same time. All participants will be in the Main Hall and all eyes will be on (COMPANY NAME) as you kick off this highly-attended panel.

Sponsorship Benefits: As sponsor of the "Brought to You By..." panel, (COMPANY NAME) will be promoted and featured via the following avenues:

□ ***T-Shirt Distribution:*** *As sponsor of the 20XX-20XX "Brought to You By..." Panel, (COMPANY NAME) shall be permitted to furnish the NSF with (COMPANY*

NAME) T-shirts during attendee registration and throughout the Conference. Note that T-shirts and (COMPANY NAME) logos require NSF approval prior to distribution.

▫ **Address the Conference:** A (COMPANY NAME) representative will be invited to address the entire conference to start Monday's "Brought to You By..." session.

▫ **Trade Show Booth:** (COMPANY NAME) will be granted one (1) double-wide 16' by 10' exhibitor's booth space as well as four (4) exhibitor registration badges to each of the upcoming three (3) NSF conferences.

▫ **Attendee Badges:** (COMPANY NAME) will also receive two (2) attendee badges to the 20XX-20XX NSF conferences.

▫ **The 20XX –20XX NSF Founders Club Sponsorship Dinner:** As mentioned in our run-down of objectives, one of the primary goals we look to help (COMPANY NAME) achieve is the creation of new industry introductions and relationships. One of the ways in which we're able to facilitate such opportunities for (COMPANY NAME) (...and our entire NSF family of sponsors), is through our private, invitation-only, NSF Founders Club dinner held in the evening preceding each year's National Sports Forum. At this dinner, we invite all of our sponsors to join with our Speakers, NSF Steering Committee members, hosts and other top VIP's in a special reception and dinner for these key individuals. As sponsor, (COMPANY NAME) will receive an invitation for two (2) to join us during those Sunday nights prior to the 20XX-20XX NSF conferences.

□ ***1/2 page Print Ad in the Official Program:*** *(COMPANY NAME) will receive space in the 20XX-20XX NSF Official Program for a 1/2 page black & white advertisement. Note that (COMPANY NAME) is required to submit their camera-ready artwork to the NSF on or before December 30th during each year of the agreement.*

□ ***Signage:*** *(COMPANY NAME) will be featured on-site at the Conference, in tandem with our other NSF sponsors with event signage (banners, signs) displaying your name and logo, and recognizing (COMPANY NAME) as an official sponsor of the Forum. NSF will produce such signage materials.*

□ ***Sponsorship Identification/Advertising:*** *As sponsor of the "Selling It..." newsletter, (COMPANY NAME) will be promoted and featured on the following 20XX-20XX NSF materials:*

Postcard Mailing: *(COMPANY NAME) will be prominently listed as a sponsor on our annual pre-event postcard sent to approximately 3,000 team sports executives in December during each year of the Agreement.*

NSF Website *(www.sports-forum.com): (COMPANY NAME) will have its logo (including a hyperlink to your website) and address information, along with a 100-word bio (provided by (COMPANY NAME)) listed on the Sponsor Page.*

E-Mail Blasts: *(COMPANY NAME) will be recognized as a sponsor of the National Sports Forum on two (2) e-mails leading up to the 20XX-20XX NSF conferences. These e-mails also reach more than 3,000 team sports executives.*

- **Use of National Sports Forum Marks:** *(COMPANY NAME) will have the right to use the NSF's copyrighted marks from the time our contract is signed until March 15, 20XX. It is recommended that (COMPANY NAME) home page include a National Sports Forum logo and reference so that visitors to the site are aware of your support of the conference and vice versa.*

- **Use of (COMPANY NAME) Marks:** *Conversely, the NSF shall be permitted to utilize and promote (COMPANY NAME) name/logo in selected promotional and advertising efforts that the NSF puts out throughout the year in advance of the next three forums.*

- **20XX-20XX NSF Steering Committee Weekend in San Diego**: *(COMPANY NAME) will receive an invitation for two (2) to join the 20XX-20XX NSF Steering Committee for our Annual "Springtime in San Diego" Board Meeting. This special weekend takes place each spring and will afford (COMPANY NAME) with an exclusive opportunity to interact with NSF Steering Committee members and other sponsors away from the Forum. Airfare and lodging courtesy of the NSF.*

Sponsorship Fee

For reasons of continuity and to appropriately leverage and recognize our sponsors over the course of the 12 months leading up to the Forum, the NSF requires a minimum of a three-year (20XX-20XX) sponsorship commitment from (COMPANY NAME) (as we do of all NSF sponsors). In return for the above-outlined sponsorship package, (COMPANY NAME) would agree to remit payment according to the following schedule:

- **Year One – 20XX:** *$XX,XXX ($YY,YYY on 4/01/XX and $ZZ,ZZZ on 9/01/XX)*

- **Year Two – 20XX:** *$XX,XXX ($YY,YYY on 4/01/XX and $ZZ,ZZZ on 9/01/XX)*

- **Year Three – 20XX:** *$XX,XXX ($YY,YYY on 4/01/XX and $ZZ,ZZZ on 9/01/XX)*

In Conclusion....

As we wrap this up here, (Name), I just wanted to again take this opportunity to thank you for your interest and your consideration in reviewing the above-outlined sponsorship proposal. Our entire staff is looking forward to the Forum continuing its growth into 20XX and beyond, and we would welcome your involvement. We have been excited to watch the Forum nearly **double in size** *over the past two years, and we anticipate considerable growth in the future as word spreads about this unique event.*

We'd most definitely welcome the opportunity to work with you and (COMPANY NAME) as part of our sponsorship family. From my end, let me give you a few days to digest all this at which time I'll be back to you to follow-up. In the meantime, please accept our best wishes and our hopes that we'll soon be working together.

Sincerely,
THE NATIONAL SPORTS FORUM

Name
Title
(800) 232-3133

We've had really good response to our proposals over the years. For one thing, they are highly customized. We don't shotgun out mass proposals into the market either. Granted, folks do. But, in my opinion, nothing could be worse than a mass-produced generic "To Whom it May Concern" type of proposal. We're after—and we're not afraid to ask for—some big money here. Plus, we're very selective as to whom we reach out to and whom we invite in to our sponsorship family. To that, I think the least we can do is handcraft every proposal we send out. I advise you to do likewise.

Homework Assignment: *Your next homework assignment is to take one of your prospects and copy our proposal formula.*

NOTE: Since putting this chapter together, I've had folks ask me if there isn't maybe a proposals-to-success ratio that they should look for in going out after this?

I wish I could give you a hard-n-fast number, but I can't. Remember, this is a "numbers game," and a lot of your success is going to depend on how well you do your homework and how well you do your prospect research.

If you've done your due diligence, asked the right questions in your introductory meeting with your prospect, and listened to what your prospect had to say, you should have a very high success ratio. After all, your event, your herd and the components you've built into your proposal should be a marvelous fit for the stated objectives of your prospective sponsor.

I don't get them all, certainly not. But for me to go to the proposal stage, that means I have a pretty good feel for what the sponsor is looking for, and I build my proposal accordingly. Do likewise and you'll be favorably pleased at how many times you'll hear: "You've got a DEAL!"

Chapter Thirteen

"CHASE Them... Until They CATCH You!"

CHASE Them...Until They CATCH You!

I grew up in New Hampshire as the only boy sandwiched between four sisters, so I got quite an ear-full about the "ways of women" and how they craftily pursued the male of the species. (I gotta say, it was pretty interesting...)

Back then, and being from an "earlier generation," it was not considered appropriate for a proper young lady to aggressively pursue a young man. That was highly frowned upon. But that didn't mean that my sisters were content to simply sit around and hope the phone would ring. Not a chance. They learned to perfect the art of what they called, "chase him...until he catches you."

They were pretty darn good at it, and I have to admit, there's some real merit in what they did and how they did it!

And although I'm sure they didn't think I was paying attention, I was. And what I learned from them I carried with me years later into the professional world. It worked for them in terms of catching guys, and I've found that it works pretty well for me in terms of catching sponsors!

Their strategy was based on being attentive, but not being overt. Interested, without being overly aggressive. Subtle, never blatant. And it plays into the philosophy that sponsorship sales is a marathon, and not a sprint.

Over the years I've long kept my sisters' "keep it cool" philosophy in mind when it comes to selling sponsorships both for myself and when teaching my sales reps the ropes. Not to say that I've found all of my sales reps to be the same. They're as distinct as different sets of fingerprints. From the "strong silent types" to the eager "yappy puppies," I've worked with them all.

And the same can be said as well for your sponsors. They too come in all shapes 'n' sizes. From the know-it-alls to the folks who say next-to-nothing and just stare at you while you make your pitch. (Both of those "kinds" can be pretty unnerving, and my advice to you is to be prepared for anything.)

And speaking of being prepared, not only does that go for your salespeople, it also goes for you, the boss. Learn to read your prospect and adjust your style to reflect that of the person you're selling. If your prospect is the buttoned-down type, it's not going to serve your purpose too well to come in there with your guns blazing! The key is to get a feel for your prospect's personality and adjust accordingly.

NOTE: If you're reading this thinking, "I'm not a sales rep! I hate to sell!" know that you couldn't be more wrong. Maybe you're not the one on your staff in charge of sales, but, believe me, if you're in business, you're in sales! In fact, you're no doubt the best salesperson your company has. You have to be to stay in business. Whether it's opening up the dialogue with a prospective client or sponsor, or convincing your bankers to extend your company's credit line, you're always selling. So get used to it and learn to get comfortable with it.

Now, your sales personality aside, let's turn the focus back to your staff and the building of your sales team.

As I said above, while maybe you can't manage your prospect's personalities, you certainly can do something about the sales reps you employ. A good rep can be worth his or her weight in gold—and a bad rep can absolutely kill your company's reputation.

Four Magic Ingredients

In fact, over the years of working with sponsorship sales people, I've managed to boil success and failure into four "magic ingredients." That said, the four things I've found in every successful sales person are:

- **The successful salesperson is always in control** – There's a profound difference between being seen as deliberate and being perceived as desperate. You can recognize a deliberate sales person—they tend to carry themselves with a sense of purpose. You invariably find them to be active, calculated, and either moving forward or moving on.

  Desperate sales people on the other hand, are often their own worst enemy. They tend to be scattered, undisciplined, lack follow through and creativeness. Big on excuses, low on results.

  I've been around both the deliberate and the desperate and I can tell you, the sales person who has their game plan worked out and systematically follows up and follows through shines through like a diamond ring every time.

- **They make sure they always have plenty of options** – A winning sales rep doesn't run out of leads. They make sure of that. They set aside time every day—either before the "traditional" work day begins or during the last hour of every afternoon to "reload their cannons," refresh their prospect lists, and update the histories on the ones they're working.

  Let's face it, with some 350 million Americans living in this country—and seemingly just as many companies out there—we should never run out of people to talk to! Sales are nothing more than a numbers game—the more prospects you have, the more opportunities you have to make a sale.

So, if you want to sell <u>one</u> sponsorship, it's simple, go after <u>ten</u> prospects.

- **Have a plan of attack** - There's an old adage that teaches "plan your work, and work your plan" and that's indeed sage wisdom. Successful sales reps set goals for themselves and then systematically go about securing those goals.

- And, above all, **they *always* keep their antenna up** - Sponsorship sales is an on-going process and therefore, if you want to sell them you need to be ever-alert to new sponsorship possibilities. Keep abreast of magazine articles, newspaper stories, leads from friends, press releases, and what's going on out at other conferences and meetings.

Follow-Up Strategies

Okay, you've got your sales head on straight and everyone focused in the right direction. You've had your initial meetings, your sponsorship proposals are out there, and you are now ready to start chasing 'em down.

For some strange reason, this chase, and the negotiations that follow, are my two favorite parts of the whole process. I love the challenge. I love being able to listen to what a prospect needs and what they want to accomplish, and then go back and create a program that takes what we already have in place or creates something entirely new that will satisfy those needs perfectly.

I think chasing sponsors down is fun, and I hope you enjoy it too. I think one reason why I enjoy this process so much is because I've got "the chase" down to a system—I have a plan and I work the plan.

First Follow-up – Personally speaking, unless my lead time is short, or I sense that my prospect is seemingly anxious to move forward, I tend to eschew sending my introductory letters through e-mail and instead use the U.S. Post Office. I like being able to have my introductory letters and follow-up proposals printed out on Sports Forum letterhead that has all the names of the steering committee running down one side of the cover sheet. It makes a pretty impressive statement without me having to say a word.

I also like having the ability to enclose some colorful "extras" in with my introductory letter. A copy of our most recent official program or our latest alumni newsletter. A four-color reprint of a magazine article or some piece of press we've recently received. Again, it's not always what you say, it's how you say it.

As you saw on both the sample introductory letter as well as the sample proposal, we tend to send our sponsorship letters/proposals out in "letter form." In other words, we compose the proposal to be, in fact, a letter from either myself or our vice president of business development, to the decision-maker we're dealing with.

The cover page of both our intro letters and our proposals are dated at the top, which in itself starts the clock running on our follow up.

I wait ten days from the date on my letter or proposal and then make my first follow-up. Experience has taught me over the years that anything earlier than ten days, and the recipient either hasn't received it yet or hasn't gotten around to reading it yet. If I wait longer than twelve days, it's out of sight, out of mind. Ten days seems to be the magic number.

It also tends to convey to the recipient that we're not desperate. And we're not. If we sell them, fine. If we don't, hey, we've lots of other people that we're talking to as well.

In some cases you get lucky and reach your decision-maker with your follow-up right off the bat. They've read it and you're ready to move forward with hopefully scheduling your first sit-down meeting in the case of the introductory letter or, in the case of the proposal, you get into their feedback.

But, much more often than not, you're apt to get a "stall." You get their voicemail or assistant. Or you get them, but they either have to (or want to...) run your proposal by some other people.

There are going to be stalls out there. It's understandable because, in our case, we're asking for a major commitment of capital and/or years. And that's fine. You learn to ride it out. But what I caution you to be sensitized to is discerning between what I call legitimate stalls and illegitimate stalls.

A legitimate stall is one where your prospect is putting you off, but you sense that they're being straight up with you about it. Their hold up could be timing related or budget approval related. If you've had a successful dialogue with your prospect up to this point, you should have a fairly good sense if they're in your corner or not in your corner on what you have put together

But more than a few times we've experienced what I'd call illegitimate stalls. They don't return your calls, or, when you do get them on the phone, they're rushed and have to call you back. Again, you just start to get a second sense about these things. You want to hang in there, but you don't want to waste your time.

I tell my staff that my favorite answer in the whole-wide world is "yes." But, barring that, my second favorite answer is "no." And my least favorite answer is anything else that's not either "yes" or "no." It's the "maybes" that will kill you.

"I'll get back to you" or "we're looking at it" or "looks good— let's talk in a few weeks"—those are the momentum killers. It's not "no," but, if you're not careful, those "maybe's" will stack up faster than the expressway at rush hour. You'll be left spinning your wheels with not much to show for it but frustration lines!

Sponsorship is a Numbers game

Your best defense in cases like this are having plenty of options or alternatives, and the two best friends a sales rep will ever have in their favor are scarcity and deadlines.

Remember, sales is a number's game. You have to have lots of prospects "in the hopper" and you have to be either moving forward or moving on to the next one.

I guess it's human nature, but I find that most people tend to not make a decision until they have to. They'll put off filing their taxes until April 15 or delay going Christmas shopping until December 24th. But you don't have all day. So what you need to grease the wheel is a little leverage. Something that makes them decide one way or the other. Enter scarcity and deadlines.

At the Sports Forum, we're like the Marines—we're looking for a "few good men." We only offer up so many sponsorships. It's limited; it's exclusive. And when we've filled our roster of eight or ten, we're done. If you want in, great, we'd love to have you. But if you're not sure, or you don't know, well, that's okay too. We'll catch you next time.

As for deadlines, sometimes the calendar creates those for you, but oftentimes, you can create them for yourself. You offer up a special discount, or you offer them a special value-added incentive or two if they can commit by the deadline.

But, whatever you do, don't allow them to just hang around. Move 'em forward—or move along.

Chapter Fourteen

"Let's Make a Deal"

A.K.A.: Everything's Negotiable

I t's bound to happen — discussions are going great with your prospect and they love what you've put together, but...

Often the "but" is over the price tag, but certainly not always. Sometimes your prospect might take issue over the payment terms, or the size of the ad you're offering them in the official program. Maybe they feel they're not getting enough registration badges in their package or feel that you should be giving them a larger trade show booth.

But whatever it is, it's keeping them from issuing those four magic words: "You've got a deal!"

The best advice I can lend to you when it comes to negotiation is to be prepared to deal with objections.

You've painstakingly put together what you think is a great proposal. You've covered their objectives with your program elements, you've included everything in the package they've asked for. But still, there's that "but"— that hesitation.

Dealing with Objections

The first thing you're going to want to do is get all the objections out on the table. And you want to do that right up front in your follow-up call or visit after you've sent out your proposal.

You get the prospect on the phone, exchange pleasantries and then get down to business with, "So, what did you think about our proposal?" Now it's your turn once again to just be quiet. Listen intently to what they have to say. In fact, it'd be a good idea to take notes.

They're bound to start by telling you what they liked. This was good (wait for it), that was great (w-a-i-t), I really liked this (it's almost there), but …" (Bingo! Now you're getting to the good stuff!)

They didn't like this, or the price is too high, or they want more of this and that. Good. The best thing you can do right now is to encourage your prospect to talk it out. You want them to tell you anything and everything they didn't like about your package. The worst thing you can do right now is to get defensive.

Why? After all, isn't it only natural to want to defend yourself? Don't. Instead, let your prospect go on. Don't cut them off or start to "argue" with them. You don't want to shut them down. Once you do that, the discussion invariably dries up, they don't buy, and you're left wondering what happened.

A better tact to take is to let them expound on what it was they found objectionable. Help them to express themselves and ask solid non-defensive questions.

Once they're finished, encapsulate what it was they just told you. You do this to make sure that: a) you got it all, b) you understood what their issues were with those objections, and c) you want to make sure they understood you were listening to them.

But don't only parrot back the objections. Also replay for them the things in the package they did like.

> "So let me see if I correctly captured the main points you just made, Mr. Smith. You loved the idea of serving as the presenting sponsor of our welcome luncheon and really liked the idea of having your company recognized as the 'host' of our post-event photo gallery on the associations' web site.

However, on the flip-side, you felt that our suggested booth location for you in the trade show hall wasn't close enough to the main flow of traffic, you're needing a couple of extra badges, and the $30,000 price tag is more than you were prepared to spend."

"Was there anything else?"

And then listen up. I call this the "speak now or forever hold your peace" part of the negotiation. I want to get it all down right in front of me and not leave the door open for them to come back with, "and another thing...," later on down the road.

From there, it's simply a matter of dealing with objections. In any negotiation, there's bound to be points of conflict. After all, you want to go one way and they want to go another. The key to all this is to never take it personally and to never let it get personal. For either of you.

There are sure to be times when you think they're being unreasonable, and no doubt they're going to be sitting there on the other side of the table thinking that you're being inflexible.

But in the end it's important for both of you to keep your eye on the prize, and that's to get this deal done.

Here's what you want to do with objections...

- **Prioritize them** – Not every objection is destined to be a deal-breaker. They're going to be some objections that are bigger roadblocks than others. Certain objections are going to fall into the "gotta haves" category and others are "nice to haves." Your mission then is to figure out which objections are which. Which ones are the biggest hurdles—and which ones they can learn to live with?

- **Test them for validity** – Hand-in-glove with the prioritization is the need to test Mr. Smith's objections for validity. Some negotiators like to throw a few red herrings out there. They'll say they don't like "x," but in reality, what's really troubling them is "y."

You test for validity by asking such questions as, "Okay, Mr. Smith, if we can get you a trade show space by the front door, are you prepared to say 'yes' to our offer?"

What you need to do is figure out where the deal-breakers are and separate those from the "nice to haves." You accomplish this by asking pointed questions. In this particular case you're not saying to Mr. Smith that you're going to move his trade show booth—you're only asking him that if you do move the booth, do we have a deal?

- **Massage them** – The more information you have about their expressed objections the clearer your path to success becomes. And you can accomplish this again by asking questions. For instance, they say that they're not prepared to pay you $30,000 for your proposed package. Your response to that should be, "Okay, what would you be prepared to pay for this package?"

I'm not suggesting that you drop your prices; all I'm encouraging you to do is learn where the ceiling is from the floor. If they respond that they only have $25,000 to spend with you, that's one thing. If, however, they answer your question by saying that they've budgeted $5,000, well, that's quite another matter altogether.

A Few Words About Budgets

Since we're talking about the price tag, which is invariably the "biggie" for both sides of the negotiation, let's take a minute here to talk about your sponsorship fee.

In a perfect world, you address their budget right up front in your initial meeting (or phone conversation). As you're 7/8's of the way through your sales call, after finishing your discussion about their sales goals and your event, you'll discuss your sponsorship packages and some of the various things you do for your sponsors. It's at this point that you should turn to your prospect and ask, "So, what kind of a budget do I have to work with in terms of putting a sponsorship package together for you?"

I can almost guarantee you that they'll return your smile and say something innocuous such as, "Well, we don't really have a budget allocated for this."

You do need to ask this question however. And if they deflect your inquiry, press forward with, "Well, what kind of a range would I have to work with for something like this?"

You really don't want to leave that first meeting without both sides having some idea as to what the costs are going to be to sponsor your event. Not bringing this up is a guaranteed recipe for disaster.

For me, I tend to nip the whole cost issue in the bud right at the outset of the discussion with our prospects. Once we start going down the sponsorship discussion road, I tell them right up front that sponsoring our event is a three-year commitment minimum and that our packages start at $25,000 for the first year.

If they leave skid marks in their haste to get out of my office, great—at least I haven't wasted either of our respective time. I'd just as soon get that out on the table right up front so that there'll be no "sticker shock" down the road.

Now having told you this, do know that if they can't afford our sponsorship price, we do have other options for them. For us they can become a platinum vendor or they can sponsor one of our continuity programs. They can sponsor one of our smaller events, be an advertiser, or just buy a trade show booth. We'll find a place for them, but I'd like to have some idea what road to point them towards coming out of my first sales call.

Trade Offs

There's an old saying in baseball that goes, "You can tell when a trade is really fair. It's when both sides walk away from the table unhappy."

And while that might very well be true in player trades, it's not necessarily the rule in sponsorship negotiation. In truth, neither side of your negotiation might come away completely thrilled, but as long as you keep your wits about you, bend, but don't break, and keep your eye on those things that are most important to you, you'll survive just fine.

Negotiations are about handling and managing trade offs. It's backing off on some of your requests so that you can advance others. It's being flexible, and it's learning how to be creative.

> *Flexible:* Nothing goes over worse than a person standing there with their arms folded across their chest shaking their head and saying "No...no...no..." to everything that comes out of your mouth.

In every successful negotiation there's got to be some "give and take." And you need to be willing to look at the equation from the other person's point of view. Ask questions as to why they're asking for what they're asking. Perhaps there's an easier way to enable them to accomplish what it is they're looking for? Or perhaps there's an equally effective alternative? But you won't know if you don't probe.

The question that often comes to mind where it comes to being flexible is "How can I make you laugh, without making me cry?"

By asking questions and trying to see the other party's point of view, you might see that an adjustment here and a tweak there can make it so that both sides are comfortable.

Creative: Tweaks and adjustments are just two other names for being creative. You've got to be willing to move some blocks around in an effort to get to "yes" if you hope to successfully skirt around the sticking points.

Let's say, for example, your sponsorship fee is a major stumbling point. You've got to find out whether they think it's too much money because they think it's worth what you're asking or they don't see the return on investment? Or is it that they just don't have the money right now?

If what you suspect is that the other party just doesn't think what you're offering is worth the price you're asking, you need to back up a bit and go back in and re-sell them.

The best way to do that is to illustrate all the great opportunities they're going to get as a result of joining your sponsorship family, to get their products/services out in front of your participants. Help them to see, and calculate, the up-side of what their future revenues might be as a result of being involved, featured, and presented in front of your group.

If they're still not seeing the return-on-investment, perhaps you need to put a little of your skin in the game. Depending on where you are and how far apart you are on the money, maybe you reduce their fee going in but take a percentage of the new business sales generated by the sponsor out of your group? If you're right about the value of your sponsorship, you might very well walk away with even more money as a result of taking a percentage than you would have when you simply asked for a flat sponsorship fee.

And as for not having the money right now, that obstacle might be as solvable as simply breaking up the other party's payment dates. Perhaps what they can agree to do is give you half down now at the time they sign the contract with the balance due broken down over two or three payments leading up to your event.

NOTE: A word of caution here. I always advise my clients to be sure that even if you break up the payments over time, always be sure that you're 100% paid in full before your conference, seminar, training program, or event. Once your event is over, you've lost all leverage over your sponsor to get paid.

And one last word about "trade-offs," know where your "hard costs" are and do your trading off accordingly. At the Sports Forum, for example, it's one thing to negotiate on the size of a program ad. Doing so doesn't necessarily raise or lower our costs significantly. We're going to print a program regardless. But adding a couple more coffee breaks or giving the sponsor an extra trade show booth, that's something else.

On the first one, adding coffee breaks, that carries with it a very real cost. With what hotels are charging these days for a cup of joe, you could send your kids to college! So acquiescing to your prospect's desires to get some added visibility by having their name plastered all over a couple extra coffee breaks carries with it a hard dollar cost to you. You have to ask yourself, is it worth it to get your sponsor to the bottom line?

As to the second example above, throwing in an extra trade show booth, this one isn't so much about adding cost as it is about sacrificing potential revenue. If your trade show hall is running "light" (in other words, sales of booth spaces aren't exactly setting the world on fire), that's one thing. If that's what they need to get the deal done—go for it.

But if you're in a smaller hall, or you know you stand an excellent chance to sell out your exhibit spaces, giving up an extra booth, while not necessarily costing you money, like the extra coffee breaks will, still takes additional revenues out of your pocket.

So know what your concessions will cost you—one way or the other and act accordingly. Not to say that you don't ultimately make the decision to move forward with their requests, but maybe you can substitute non expense/revenue concessions (i.e. additional attendee badges, product sampling, and flyer distribution) for those that will cost you.

When you get to this point, it's vital to have a thorough understanding of your hard costs so you are better prepared to negotiate.

Set Your Parameters Going In

To be truly happy coming out, you need to have a pretty solid idea of where you want to be going in.

To do that you need to establish for your organization reasonable sponsorship goals/ objectives going in. Doing so will enable you to have a pretty good idea of where you can bend and where you can't in your upcoming negotiations.

The operative word I've used above is setting "reasonable" goals. I'm often surprised by how crazy people can get here. For instance, one of the first questions I ask my sponsorship consulting clients is what their sponsorship dollar objectives are? They'll invariably give me a number to which I respond, "Great, and where are your sponsorship dollar numbers now?"

If there's a radical jump in those two numbers, I need to press for more detail. "Let's see, you're setting the bar at $100,000 in sponsorships next year; however, what you're also telling me is that you've averaged $20,000 in sponsorships in each of the past three years?"

If they answer in the affirmative, I have to ask, "So if you don't mind telling me, what is it that you were planning on doing to raise this coming year's sponsorship five times higher than they've been in the past three years?"

I'm not saying that they're wrong, or that they can't do it. I'm just wanting to see whether they have their feet on the ground or not. Maybe they're planning on rolling out some new events, or changing their format, or expanding their audience? I don't know.

But then again, maybe they're just throwing a number out there and hoping that if they say it, they'll earn it!

As I see it, my job with my clients is to help them focus and tap into some outstanding dollars that exist in this all-too-neglected revenue stream. Most folks I talk to aren't generating any dollars from selling sponsorship to their herd, and when they get introduced to the "wonderful world of sponsorship" they get stars in their eyes.

I'm not here to rain on anyone's parade, but I think it's important right from the outset to establish clear, reasonable overall sponsorship revenue expectations and then break that number down into the many different "pieces" (different sponsorable inventory) that, when added together, will get you to that "big number."

Once you break that big number down into its individual component pieces, you will then know what kind of parameter, or range, you can work with in selling each of your sponsorship packages.

That way, when you go into your negotiation, you have a definitive idea of how much — or how little—you can move off your asking price. Maybe in the end you don't get all the dollars you wanted for a particular piece of inventory, but perhaps, in getting to the deal, you moved out some hard dollar costs involved. You took in less money, but your costs were also reduced, so in the end, you still did okay.

The goal, as we established in the outset of this section, is to establish and set your objectives, your parameters going in so that you can negotiate smarter, more profitable packages for your organization.

"Yes, But..."

This is a term we use in my company for dealing with sponsor requests during our negotiations. It doesn't stand for "Yes, but..." as in we're arguing or debating with our clients. We don't generally advise trying to debate your way to "yes."

No, rather what we mean by "Yes, but..." is that we do our best to accede to our sponsor's requests, but, in so doing, letting them know right up front that there will be a cost to do so. Again, it's about trade offs.

Not that we do this on everything. A lot of times, in the spirit of flexible negotiation, we're able to gladly satisfy our prospect's request. But generally speaking, we strive to offer up a fair, targeted package for a fair sponsorship fee in return.

There are still times when we are asked for something that we didn't anticipate or can't easily, affordably accommodate. In such cases, what we strive to do is give the sponsor what they're asking for, but trade it for something we'll want or need in return.

Yes, some of the time what we're going to need in return is more money. I don't mind asking for it. For instance, that sponsor who wants two additional coffee breaks added to our event? "Yes, we'll do that, but we're going to need to bump your sponsorship fee up accordingly." "Yes, but."

Sometimes it's not a money issue, but something else entirely. I mentioned previously that we only sell our sponsorships on three-year minimum commitments. That's pretty unusual in the meeting industry and oftentimes it catches our prospects up short.

"I don't think we're comfortable committing to three years," you'll often hear them say.

"Well," I respond, "while we have some sponsors committed to us for five years, for continuity reasons, and because we're able to do more for our sponsors on a 12-month a year basis, we ask our sponsors for a minimum of a three year commitment."

"But what if I don't like the results of this association after the first year, and I want to get out?"

"We would, of course, be disappointed," I respond, "because we try to do everything in our power to keep our sponsors happy and contented with us. But I can certainly understand your concern. So here's what I would propose." (Be creative.) "How about if we set up your contract with us such that your company will be given a limited window of opportunity after the first full year of your sponsorship—let's say 60-days immediately following the conclusion of our conference—in which you can contact us, say you want to terminate the remaining two years of the contract, and you can walk away completely free and clear? Is that fair?"

Usually they'll agree that what you have proposed is more than fair.

"But," I continue, "We would ask that we be given the same window of opt-out opportunity to negate the final two years of our contract as well. Deal?"

You might be reading this wondering, "Why would you want to get out of a three year deal?"

That's certainly a legitimate question, and one answer to it is that having a "no-fault" opt-out clause can work in your favor in the event that market conditions should change. For instance, it's possible that your event doubles in size over the following two years, and puts you in a position to be able to charge significantly more for your sponsorships. Or perhaps you decide that the special panel session that "XYZ Company" annually underwrites is no longer a red hot topic to your attendees. Without an out-clause you'd be forced to continue offering the session because you've sold the entitlement to it to a sponsor.

Those are possibilities, but in complete candor, in all my years of selling multi-year sponsorships to the Sports Forum, I've only pulled the plug twice on an on-going multi-year sponsorship in place. And both times it had everything to do with the personality of the sponsor and how difficult they were to work with. In neither case did it have anything to do with market conditions. If we make a deal, we'll honor it. But we won't work with a pain in the butt. We do try our best, but sometimes you just have to "fire" your sponsors.

Now, having shared this with you, I need to tell you that generally we don't as a rule, go into a multi-year sponsorship discussion requesting an opt-out clause. If the other side asks for one, however, we're more than happy to accede to their request so long as they agree to extend the opt-out opportunity to us as well.

Usually this stops the other side cold.

They want the opportunity to walk away, but, generally speaking, they don't want us to be allowed to do likewise. Oftentimes what's running through their minds and they might even say so out loud, "Wait a minute…what's to say that one of my competitors doesn't come along once they learn about this show and offer you more money to cut us loose and let them be your sponsor?"

"That's a very real possibility." I tell them, "But that's the risk you'd have to be willing to take. After all, fair is fair, right?"

You might be wondering if we've ever had a sponsor pull the plug on us? And the answer is, "Yes, twice." I'm happy to say though that neither time was the result of poor execution or faulty representation on our part. One of the two "walk-a-ways" was the result of one of our sponsoring companies deciding that their future wasn't in pursuing sales through the sports arena, so the Forum audience wasn't one they wished to pursue any further. And the second walk-away was a company that was having money problems—problems that resulted in them ultimately closing their doors.

But those are "Yes, buts" as it pertains to multi-year contracts. A lot of times the "Yes, but" will be about the money you're asking for. Perhaps your prospect has come at you looking to hammer you down on the fee you're asking for. Let's say, for instance your asking price is $25,000, but your prospect only wants to pay $20,000.

In that case, your "Yes, but" could be,

"Yes, we could see our way clear to reducing your sponsorship package price to $20,000. I think if we take out the trade show booth, and reduced your two sponsored coffee breaks to one, that would enable us to recapture the revenue by selling your space to someone else, and we could secure another sponsor for that second coffee break. Will that work for you?"

You see what I'm doing here? It's not, "No, we couldn't discount our price by 20 percent." It's "Sure, we'll get to your number. Here's how we'll do it!"

Be creative, be flexible, and be fair. And expect the same in return.

The Nibblers

This is one of those things that can really turn a good relationship sour in a hurry. You'll run into these folks from time to time, and the best advice I can give to you is to cut it off at the neck —fast.

Nothing makes me happier than to offer up some added value to a sponsor completely at random. We subscribe to a philosophy of under-promise and over-deliver. It keeps sponsors happy and coming back for more.

But every now and then you run into a sponsor who is constantly asking you for more, more, more. No matter what you do, you can't seem to make them happy. No matter what you give them, it's never enough. You can help yourself, right up front, by making sure you get out all of their needs, asks, and demands right up front in the negotiation. You ask them, "Is there anything else?"

You take their final roster of needs, affix your fair price, and deliver them back a final contract or letter of agreement. You're done, right?

Well, not always. No sooner do you have a signed deal than they start asking you for a couple more registration badges, or that black and white half-page ad, could you bump that up to a full-page four-color?

We call these guys nibblers, always nibbling for more than they agreed to. Your initial inclination is to give them what they ask for. After all, you want to keep them happy. But, in the end, fair is fair and enough is enough. And that's how you nip this in the bud. You appeal to the sponsor's sense of fairness.

"C'mon," you say. "You guys negotiated one heck of a good package with us. We put together a great sponsorship for you at a fair price. But everything was based on your paying "x" for receiving "y." Now you're asking for two more of these and an increase in that. We can do this, of course, but we're going to have to adjust your sponsorship fee accordingly."

Generally, that will stop it. And stop it you should. We coach you to be fair, but we're not encouraging you to be a doormat! And don't you be guilty of this either. You make a deal, you stick to it.

The Power to Walk Away

And the last thing I want to talk about before we move on to contracts and letters of agreement is to advise you to always go into a negotiation fully prepared and completely willing to get up and walk away from the table. You need to be able to smile, thank the other person and tell them that unfortunately you don't think you're going to be able to be of service to them. And leave.

Don't ever put yourself in a position where you have to get the deal done at any cost. That's not a negotiation, that's a donation! Admittedly a lot of times you'll find yourself getting caught up in the moment. You've worked hard to get to this point and, dang it, you want to get this deal done. But remember, sponsorship is a marathon, not a sprint. To win, you've got to run all 26.2 miles...not 20, 24 or 25. All the way.

If you're not fully able to call the game when you clearly recognize that getting to a deal won't be a good deal for you, then you're headed for trouble.

Go into every negotiation absolutely willing to give the other party a great return for a solid investment. You're building a partnership here with your sponsors and you don't take that lightly.

But by establishing your parameters, your goals, going in—and recognizing what things cost you—you start out from a strong position. Don't sacrifice that strength by giving away the store. If it's not right, walk away. If you're planning your work and working your plan, you should have plenty of other prospects that you can talk to in addition to the one you're negotiating with right now.

Either move forward...or move on.

And with that, let's close the chapter on negotiation. Truly you could write an entire book on the strategies of negotiation—and, in fact, several zillion books on the subject exist out there!

But with a little practice and armed with the knowledge that the property you represent is truly of value, you will more times than not walk out of every negotiation with a smile on your face, some incremental dollars in your bank, and with a partnering sponsor that you can help make rich.

It's a "win-win" all the way around, and, in my book, those are the best deals to shoot for out there.

Chapter Fifteen

"Write It Up..."

The Deal's Not Done...Until the Paperwork is Finished

How's this for a recipe for disaster?

I ran into a good sponsor friend of mine a few years ago who shared with me a story that still has me shaking my head. Her employer, a well-known bank, had agreed to sponsor a professional ball club and went into the new season with high expectations for success. The negotiations had gone back and forth during the pre-season but ultimately, with both sides agreeing to make concessions, they had emerged with a six-figure deal she thought was both fair and effective.

About halfway through the season her contact person at the ball club left suddenly. In talking over the bank's sponsorship package with the new club marketing head, she realized that a number of things her rep had promised her the team would do simply weren't getting done.

She pressed the new marketing director about this and learned, to her chagrin, that the new marketing head had no knowledge of a good half-dozen of his predecessor's concessions. You see there weren't any records. Instead, stuck on the back of file folders, was a number of little yellow "stickies" with cryptic notes scrawled on them. However, stickies aside, without anything official and concrete, the ball club had failed to make good on a series of agreements and promises. This, as you can imagine, caused a great deal of embarrassment all the way around, not to mention a half-season's worth of "make goods" the club owed the bank the following season.

That's really a shame, but it's not the first time a good relationship has unraveled because one side or the other failed to properly execute the paperwork.

So my advice to you is not to learn this lesson the hard way. Always remember that no sale is ever finished until the paperwork is complete! (And, on the sponsor's side, don't ever assume you have an agreement until you've seen it in writing.)

And the most important of these documents is, of course, the contract.

I'm Not a Lawyer, But...

Now before I say anything more about contracts, Letters of Agreement ("LoA") or anything else even *remotely* legal...let me first make this disclaimer: I am not a lawyer nor have I ever studied law. What I'll be expressing here are strictly my opinions—one of which is that I would strongly encourage you to seek out the advice of your own legal representatives in preparing, finalizing and signing anything legally binding.

And where sponsorship agreements are concerned, the deal should definitely be contained, specified and acknowledged in a writing signed by both parties.

When you come right down to it, despite all the letters, e-mails and notes you and your sponsor may have exchanged, the signed contract or LoA will control what happens. If ever you find yourself having to go to court, the contract is, generally speaking, the document that usually trumps everything else. Here is what my advisors tell me: any negotiations that took place before the contract or LoA was executed are typically inadmissible in court to prove the terms of the contract or LoA or to contradict, vary, or add to the writing. Although there are a few narrow exceptions to this general rule, it is imperative that all terms and agreements between the parties are included in the signed contract or LoA. Furthermore, any additions or changes to the contract or LoA which are made after the contract has been signed should also be noted and contained in a signed writing.

Sponsorships are, after all, built almost entirely on trust. Your sponsor representative trusts you, your company, what you can do for them and your word. Without that basic level of trust, nothing else is worth a dime.

But what often happens in deals that ultimately go "sideways" is that layers of miscommunication or misunderstanding have occurred. What you thought they said, or what they thought you meant, don't match up. Many times you can fix this and make it "right" for the other party. But sometimes the damage is so severe that one, or both, parties decides that their only recourse is to litigate. It's in those situations that the law is going to cut through what both sides thought they said to get at what both sides literally signed, sealed and delivered: the contract.

Again, I'm not a lawyer, but when it comes to contracts, it basically comes down to both parties stipulating what each side is going to do in your agreement. To this there are some basic elements that all agreements should contain:

NOTE: Identification of the parties, a breakdown of the subject matter of the agreement, the exchange, and signatures are absolutely required to make a contract or LoA legally binding. The other elements that are listed are not required but should be included for clarity.

- **Clear identification of all parties** – In most situations there are only two parties represented, your company and the other guy's. However, there are certainly instances where there may be multiple parties, individuals and/or corporations involved in the deal. Sometimes this will result in a number of separate contracts by and between all the involved organizations and other times it may result in a single document recognizing all of the multiple parties and signed by authorized representatives of each. However you structure it, in your contract, you should make sure that all the parties bound to your particular agreement are identified.

  NOTE: Make sure you get each party's legal name listed in the agreement. In our case, The National Sports Forum is a subsidiary of our legal name, Seaver Marketing Group, Inc. Therefore in our contracts and LoAs, I notate and identify each in my Sports Forum agreements.

- **A break down of everything each party agrees to do/provide** – As you know, lawyers tend to charge a lot of money—and this is one area in which they earn their keep. A good lawyer will oftentimes go in the direction of specificity foregoing brevity over detail. They'll break down the subject matter of your agreement into a thorough series of specific actions, rights and entitlements that both sides have agreed to furnish the other notating not only such things as elements, quantities and deliverables, but also deadlines for action and rights. The result frequently makes for tough reading, but in the final analysis, both sides should clearly specify what it is they have promised to do for the other.

- **The exchange** – A contract or LoA must include what the other party agrees to either do or provide for you in exchange for the performance of your promise. In other words, a contract should specify the compensation your organization is to receive in return for your keeping up your end of the bargain. If it's money, great—how much and what are the agreed upon payment terms? If there are products and/or services to be provided in return, clearly and thoroughly list what those are to be as well, including when they are to be delivered.

- **Late fees** – I would further recommend that you include a section which specifies your late fee policies when payment/ deliveries are not received on time. This section should outline when late fees are charged and in what amounts.

- **Recourse** – I also recommend that you add a section or two on what action you're both agreeing to take if either (or both) side feels that your agreement has been violated and you can't come to a mutually-suitable resolution. For instance, do you both agree to forego legal action in favor of binding arbitration? Or do you both agree to use a mediator to help settle a dispute? Arbitration is conducted by a neutral third-party who decides a dispute and can be either binding or non-binding. Arbitration is a good alternative to litigation because it will generally save you both a lot of time as well as legal fees. Mediation can serve as a first step to help reconcile a dispute before parties resort to arbitration or litigation. Mediation, which is often recommended by courts, merely facilitates an opportunity for both parties to come to a mutually agreed upon resolution. However, if you want your discrepancies to be dealt with through a court of law you should specify such in the contract and also stipulate what state your agreement should be adjudicated in, thereby providing the state laws which will control your contract. The city and state where the arbitration and/or mediation is to take place should also be listed in this section.

- **Limitations on liability** – I also recommend that you include a section specifying liability limitations and restrictions to protect your company as well as its directors, officers, and owners. This section should state the extent of liability and/ or indemnification, which parties are covered and in what circumstances.

- **Entirety of the writing** – I would also recommend that you include a section which specifies that the signed contract sets forth the entire agreement of the parties. You may also want this section to further add that any modifications or amendments to the contract must be attached to and specifically incorporated into the contract by the initials of each party and dated by each party. If you decide to rewrite the contract some time in the future, it is critical to note that all prior writings are heretofore revoked and that the current writing represents the entire agreement.

- **Signed and dated** – With all elements clearly mapped out and stipulated, you must conclude your agreement with lines at the end for both parties to sign and date. I always put blank lines for both parties to sign with each party's name below the line because signatures are oftentimes not all that legible! Below that I put a line for both parties to write in their title. Obviously it's imperative that both signing parties are legally authorized to represent their organization. Below that I type in both party's official title. And lastly I put in a blank line for each to write in the date they have signed the agreement with the words "Date of Agreement" written below that bottom line.

I think that pretty much covers it. But again, I would encourage you to retain the services of a reputable lawyer to help you to draft/ look over your finished product.

Changes in the Contract/Agreement – Oftentimes there are going to be some minor changes in your agreement. Perhaps it involves a date for a deliverable or a quantity change. If there are major changes or a number of minor discrepancies, you'd often be wise to scrap your original draft in favor of rewriting the agreement. As noted above, if a new contract is written, it must acknowledge that all prior writings are revoked and that the current writing represents the entire agreement. If, however, the changes are relatively minor and few in number, it's legally permissible for you to strike through the changes in pen, make the revised change and have both sides initial and date those changes. (NOTE: Anything crossed out, added, revised or modified in any way that is not initialed and dated by both sides from the original document may not be legally binding. Rule of thumb: When in doubt, initial and date.)

Letters of Agreement vs. Contracts – A Letter of Agreement (LoA) is a type of contract that is written more in letter form. Personally I tend to opt for LoAs in our agreements because they tend not to come across so official. They're both binding—both identify the parties involved, both list what the parties agree to do in the transaction, both specify the exchange, and both are signed and dated by all parties involved.

Here is a copy of one of our LoAs – so you can see how we write up one of our deals. Obviously what I'm including herein is fictitious; the names (aside from our own) are fictitious as are the terms and compensation of the deal. However, what you see here is representative of what generally goes into one of our LoAs.

NATIONAL SPORTS FORUM™

September 18, 20XX

Mr. Joe Smith
President
Acme Widgets
456 32nd Avenue
Anytown, California 99999

Dear Joe,

> *20XX-20XX National Sports Forum*
> *Sponsorship Agreement by and between:*
> *Acme Widgets & Seaver Marketing Group,*
> *Inc./The National Sports Forum*

*On behalf of all of us at **Seaver Marketing Group, Inc**. ("SMG"), involved in putting on the National Sports Forum ("NSF"), we're delighted to have **Acme Widgets** join us as a sponsor of the 20XX – 20XX National Sports Forums.*

That said, please accept this letter as our Official Letter of Agreement covering the roughly three (3) year time frame from the time this agreement is signed **through May 1, 20XX.**

1. Sponsorship Components of this Agreement:

What follows is a breakout of the different components that will make up the overall sponsorship by and between SMG and Acme Widgets over the term of this Agreement:

20XX – 20XX National Sports Forum's "Ticketing Insights" Panel Sponsored by Acme Widgets:

Description: *The National Sports Forum's "Ticketing Insights" Panel is one of the Forum's signature events and has become a perennial favorite of the NSF attendees. Introduced in 20XX, this panel discussion is made up of individually selected senior-level team/event ticket sales executives who share their experience and expertise with our audience— a group comprised primarily of senior level team, event and industry executives. Because of the "Ticketing Insights" Panel's popularity, there are no other competing events going on during this panel.*

While it's still too early for us to know the dates and locations for the 20XX & 20XX NSFs, this coming year, when we're in Memphis, the "Ticketing Insights Panel" that Acme Widgets will sponsor will be held at the Peabody Hotel on **Monday, January 28, 20XX**, *in Memphis, TN.*

Sponsorship Benefits: *Acme Widgets, as part of their overall sponsorship program, shall, during each year of this Agreement, receive the following pre-and-on-site promotional components:*

- **Six (6) Attendee Badges:** *As part of this package, Acme Widgets shall receive six (6) Attendee Registration Badges for each year of this agreement.*

- **Two (2) Inner Circle Memberships:** *As part of Acme Widget's sponsorship involvement, two (2) Acme Widgets representatives will receive complimentary Inner Circle memberships in each of the three years of this agreement.*

- **Address the Conference:** *Joe Smith, or an otherwise designated representative of Acme Widgets, shall have the right to address the NSF Conference at the "Ticketing Insights Panel" prior to the panel discussion during each year of the Agreement.*

- **Collateral Material Distribution:** *Acme Widgets shall be granted the right, should they so desire, to have Acme Widgets collateral distributed to all NSF Attendees at the Acme Widgets-sponsored "Ticketing Insights Panel" during each of the three years of this Agreement. (Note: It is understood and agreed that in such cases where Acme Widgets collateral is distributed, it shall be SMG's responsibility to provide distribution and Acme Widgets to furnish the collateral to be distributed.)*

- **Break Out Session Participation:** *As part of Acme Widgets sponsorship involvement, a Acme Widgets representative shall be invited to participate as a Break Out Session moderator in each of the next three (3) upcoming National Sports Forum Conferences.*

- **The NSF's Founder's Club Sponsorship Dinner:** *As part of this Agreement, it is understood that Acme Widgets shall receive an invitation for two (2) to be a part of the annual National Sports Forum Founder's*

Club Dinner which takes place on the evening prior to the first day of each year's conference. This shall extend to all three years of this Agreement.

□ **20XX-20XX NSF Steering Committee Weekend in San Diego:** Acme Widgets shall receive an invitation for two (one Acme Widgets representative plus guest) to join the 20XX-20XX NSF Steering Committee for the Annual Springtime in San Diego Board Meeting which takes place in the spring of each year following the Forum. "Springtime in San Diego" is an exclusive window to interact with steering committee members and other sponsors away from the Forum. Airfare and lodging courtesy of the NSF.

□ **NSF Trade Show Booth:** Acme Widgets shall be granted, should Acme Widgets so desire, usage of one (1) standard size exhibitor's booth to use during all three year's of the National Sports Forum conference as covered in this Agreement. Furthermore, it is agreed that Acme Widgets booth location, again should they so desire, would be in the NSF's preferred exhibitor area reserved exclusively for sponsors of the NSF.

□ **1/2 page Print Ad in the Official Program:** Acme Widgets shall receive one half-page black & white ad space in the NSF's 20XX-20XX Official Program. (So as to enable the NSF to meet their printing deadlines, it is agreed by both parties that Acme Widgets will submit their camera-ready art to the NSF **on or before December 10th** proceeding each year of the Agreement.)

□ **On-site Signage:** Acme Widgets shall be recognized on-site at each of the 20XX-20XX National Sports Forums, with event signage (i.e. banners, signs) – displaying Acme Widgets name and logo, and *recognizing Acme Widgets as an Official Sponsor of the National Sports Forum. The NSF shall be responsible for producing all such on-site signage materials*

◻ **Sponsorship Identification/Advertising:** *As Official Sponsor of the National Sports Forum, Acme Widgets shall be promoted and featured in all of the following NSF materials. Such materials shall include:*

> **NSF Agenda Brochures**: *Acme Widgets shall be prominently listed as the Official Sponsor of the NSF's "Ticketing Insights Panel" in the 20XX-20XX NSF Agenda Brochure. Each brochure will go out to more than 3,000 team sports executives. Traditionally, Agenda brochures are mailed in late November of each year preceding the conference.*

> **NSF Attendee Brochures**: *Acme Widgets shall be recognized, in general, as an Official Sponsor of the NSF in the NSF Attendee Brochures that shall go out each summer prior to each of the last two NSF conferences covered in this Agreement.*

> **Postcard Mailing:** *Acme Widgets shall be recognized as an Official Sponsor on the NSF's lead-up postcard sent preceding each year's conference covered in this Agreement.*

> **NSF Website** *(www.sports-forum.com): Acme Widgets shall have its logo (including a hyperlink to Acme Widgets website) and address information, along with a bio (provided by Acme Widgets with the understanding and agreement that said bio not to exceed 100 words), listed on the sponsor page. In addition, Acme Widgets shall be listed on the agenda page as the presenting sponsor of the "Ticketing Insights Panel" each year of this agreement.*

E-mail Blasts: *Acme Widgets shall be recognized as a sponsor of the National Sports Forum on two (2) e-mails each year leading up to the 20XX-20XX events.*

◻ ***Use of National Sports Forum Marks:*** *As an official sponsor of the NSF, Acme Widgets shall have rights to use all NSF marks from the time the contract is signed until May 1, 20XX.*

◻ ***Use of Acme Widgets' Marks:*** *Conversely, the NSF shall have the right to use Acme Widgets' marks in the promotion/advertising of Acme Widgets involvement as a sponsor of the 20XX – 20XX NSF. This right will also expire on May 1, 20XX.*

Sponsorship Fee

In return for the above-outlined sponsorship package – which would make Acme Widgets the sponsor of the 20XX-20XX National Sports Forum's "Ticketing Insights Panel", Acme Widgets agrees to remit the following:

*Year One *– 20XX:* **$XX,XXX** *(with $XX,XXX due on or before 1/1/XX);*
*Year Two *– 20XX:* **$XX,XXX** *(with $XX,XXX due on or before 6/1/XX, $XX,XXX due on or before 9/1/XX);*
*Year Three *– 20XX:* **$XX,XXX** *(with $XX,XXX due on or before 6/1/XX, $XX,XXX due on or before 9/1/XX).*

◻ **Late Fees:** *Both sides recognize and acknowledge the importance of timely payments in the process of executing the agreed-upon elements contained within this Agreement. For this reason, Acme Widgets agrees that they shall make every effort to make their payments as laid out above on or before the appointed payment* *dates. Should however for any reason Acme Widgets payments not be received within fifteen (15) days of the above-listed payment dates, Acme Widgets agrees that they shall be accessed, and will pay to the NSF, a late payment interest penalty of 1.5% of the fee owed, compounded, for every month that their payment is not received. It is understood and agreed by both parties that late payment interest penalty shall begin on the date that the fee was initially due.*

2. Hold Harmless Clause:

In affixing their signature on the next page, Acme Widgets herein agrees to indemnify, defend and hold harmless Seaver Marketing Group and The National Sports Forum, its respective officers, Sponsors, Advertisers and Steering Committee members against all liability, claims, suits, actions, proceedings, costs, damages and expenses, including all reasonable attorney fees for the cost of defending any claims or the like, incurred by Seaver Marketing Group and The National Sports Forum directly or indirectly arising out of, based upon, related to or in connection with any breach of any of SMG/ NSF warranties or agreements set forth in this Agreement; (ii) any alleged defects or inherent dangers in the products or services by SMG/NSF; and (iii) any injuries or damages to purchasers arising from or related to products or services provided by SMG/NSF.

Conversely, Seaver Marketing Group and the National Sports Forum, shall, in affixing their signature on the next page, herein agree to indemnify, defend and hold harmless Acme Widgets, its respective officers, Sponsors, Advertisers and Steering Committee members against all liability, claims, suits, actions, proceedings, costs, damages and expenses, including all reasonable attorney fees for the cost of defending any claims or the like, incurred by Acme Widgets directly or indirectly arising out of, based upon, related to or in connection with any breach of any of Acme Widgets warranties or agreements set forth in this Agreement; (ii) any alleged defects or inherent dangers in the products or services by Acme Widgets, and (iii) any injuries or damages to purchasers arising from or related to products or services provided by Acme Widgets.

3. Disputes and Binding Arbitration:

Both parties accept that they are entering into this Agreement under mutual good faith and that any/all disagreements or disputes as to the terms of the execution of this Agreement shall be addressed and if at all possible remedied through discussion by/between both parties.

However, should suggested remedies through direct resolution not be acceptable to either/both parties, it is agreed upon by both parties that both shall enter into Binding Arbitration in order to resolve any lingering disputes.

For said arbitration, it is understood that this Agreement is governed and shall be construed under the laws of the State of California and that any arbitration brought under the terms of this Contract shall be done in the County of San Diego.

4. Entirety:

This Letter of Agreement contains the entire understanding of the parties with respect to the subject matter hereof and there are no other agreements, understandings or representations of warranties, except as expressly set forth herein.

In Conclusion...

As a sign of the acceptance of the Agreement, it is requested that both parties duly initial each page and sign in the appro-

priate place on the next page. Should there be any questions, or if you would like something additional included herein, please don't hesitate to contact me at your earliest convenience. If not, and if everything meets with your acceptance and approval, please signify by signing below. Thanks for your time and cooperation, Joe – we're very much looking forward to working with you and Acme Widgets over these next three years.

Sincerely yours
SEAVER MARKETING GROUP, INC./ THE NATIONAL SPORTS FORUM

Ron Seaver
President

In signing below, both parties are acknowledging their complete and full acceptance of all of the Terms and Conditions as laid out in this Letter of Agreement.

That said, please sign and date below to mark your acceptance and agreement with the items stated above.

AGREED AND ACCEPTED

_____   _____

Ron Seaver   **Joe Smith**
President   *President*
Seaver Marketing Group   *Acme Widgets*
(d/b/a National Sports Forum)

_____   _____

Date   **Date**

_____

And there you have it. I'm sure there're a *zillion* other contract forms you can use...but this one's the one we generally go with.

A couple final words about contracts and agreements: admittedly, they are a pain in the neck to do. They take a lot of time, require a lot of concentration and are simply something you'd rather not mess with. In a perfect world, you've got a legal department that you can dish this task off to! But unfortunately most of us don't.

Tempting as it might seem, resist the temptation to push this off. As soon as you shake hands on an agreement, get it down in writing.

And here's another recommendation. Oftentimes, in certain situations, it may be perfectly acceptable for you to have the other party be the one to prepare the contract. That's pretty tempting, isn't it? It's one less thing that you have to do! But resist. In fact, I'm going to go so far as to strongly suggest that in all situations you be the one that offers to prepare the contract.

Why?

Simple. In just about every sponsorship discussion there are apt to be certain untouched "gray areas" that don't get addressed. These are points that for any number of reasons are important but they didn't get specifically discussed. For instance, while sponsorship cost always comes up, oftentimes payment dates don't. For instance, they've agreed to pay you $50,000 for the sponsorship but neither one of you said when that money would be due. Or you agreed that the sponsor would receive a full-page ad in your program, but the art work submission deadline date didn't come up.

Who's responsible if someone gets hurt at your event? (Is the sponsor indemnified?) Is there any special pricing consideration if the sponsor should decide at the last minute they want to bring four more people to your conference? Are you paying for the sponsor's travel or that of their VIPs? Does the sponsor's logo get reprinted in four-color on your collateral or is black-and-white permissible? Is the sponsor's name listed above the name or below the name of your event? Are there any late fees or interest payments due if the sponsor doesn't pay you on the agreed upon dates stipulated in the contract?

These are just a few of the literally hundreds of things that may not come up in your sponsorship discussions. Certainly you've agreed on all the big things, but it's in all these small little details that a great relationship starts to unravel.

So don't let it. Be proactive and offer to write the contract and make sure you have your bases covered. By the way, the party that writes the contract invariably decides all these little issues to their own favor. If, for no other reason, you're going to want to make sure that party is you!

Chapter Sixteen

"It's SHOWtime!"

Putting Your ALL into Your Activation

As tedious and annoying as writing contracts can be, it's in the activation where you really earn your money. In short, activation is everything!

If you're not familiar with the term activation, it's the act and actions you and your sponsor take to make the sponsorship work for the company doing the sponsoring.

Or as the sponsorship experts, IEG put it:

The marketing activities a company conducts to promote its sponsorship. Money spent on activation is over and above the rights fee paid to the sponsored property. Also known of as leverage.

(Source: IEG's Guide to Sponsorship)

I don't know about you, but that still sounds a little vague to me. So let's try a "for instance."

Let's say as part of your deal you offer your sponsor the opportunity to give away two free year-long memberships to your association (or a couple of free registrations to your upcoming conference). That's great, but only as far as it goes. To take it to the next level somebody's got to let the sponsor's customers know that this benefit is available or it won't do anybody any good, right?

"Activation Is EVERYTHING!"

Getting word out about the sponsor's affiliation with you, and about this free registration opportunity, is activation. It's how you take the words off the proposal page and put it into action. And just as IEG said in their definition above, the cost of activating the sponsorship is frequently on top of the cost the sponsor pays to buy the rights to the association from you.

But you have activation responsibilities as well. Your sponsor has to get the word out on their end, but so do you. You've promised your sponsor you're going to do certain things for them, and now you have to do it! And it's those actions, the ones that you take in doing it is how you activate their sponsorship.

And this is critical, because how you do it, and how well you do it, often makes all the difference in whether this is a "one time thing" or if you're going to get the renewal.

I'll go more into this later, but let's touch briefly on renewals now. For me, I'm all about the renewals. As I tend to hammer into my staff at the Sports Forum, "I'm not so much interested in getting a sponsor on board for the first time as I am about getting their renewal!"

Granted there are any number of reasons—things well beyond your control—that may preclude a sponsor from coming back with you. They may discontinue the line that targeted your herd, or they could decide they want to go after a different group. They could sell their company or go out of business. Many times your decision-maker at the sponsor leaves the company and their replacement wants to go in a completely different direction with their marketing.

Those things, and more, may happen, but here's where you have to make me a promise. Promise me that you won't let a sponsor walk away from you because you failed to execute and deliver on your end.

What Activation Is ... and What It Means to Both Parties

In my experience, this is the number one reason why sponsors will invariably stop doing business with you. It's because you pretty much disappeared after you got your check. I hear this complaint constantly, time and time again from the corporate sponsors we talk to. It's truly a shame.

Remember, as I said way back in the beginning, sponsorship isn't a donation, it's a partnership. And if you're too busy, too pre-occupied to keep your sponsor's interests in mind, you should get someone on board that will. The dollars are just too big and this is just too important.

At the Sports Forum we have one person on staff whose chief responsibility is to break apart every one of our sponsorship agreements and time/duty activates each obligation. They keep separate files on each of our sponsors and maintain one master file containing overall spreadsheets of who is owed what.

Take our official program for instance. Every sponsor, platinum vendor, partner and/or advertiser who has either directly purchased an ad, or gets one included in their sponsorship package, is listed on our program spreadsheet. Included on the spreadsheet are the specifications of each ad: full size, half-page, full-color or black-and-white, inside cover, or special placement within the program. When is their artwork deadline due to us? Did we send them their one-month-to-deadline reminder and our two-weeks-out reminder? Who's the ad contact person and their contact information? Are there any other special agreements, arrangements and/or benefits due to our advertiser/sponsor? For instance, perhaps, as part of the deal, the advertiser/sponsor gets a couple attendee badges? And who, at the advertiser or sponsor is your attendee contact person?

For obvious legal reasons you really don't want to drop the ball on making sure that you deliver on what you've promised. But more than that, failure to execute can absolute kill your ability to attract new sponsors. Believe me, this is a small world and word of your inability to follow-through can and will get around.

So stay alert. Not only dedicate yourself to delivering what you've promised, but wherever and whenever you can, over-deliver. Give them more than what you promised them. Trust me, in a world where folks are used to fighting for everything they're owed, your willingness to go the extra mile will be recognized and appreciated. So take care of the geese that lay the golden eggs, and you will be rewarded with happy contented sponsors that come back year after year!

And know, as you set about the task of sponsorship execution, that this may sound simpler than it is. As you start to get larger and begin attracting more sponsors, keeping tabs on everything can definitely become a daunting task. For instance, when I was at the Padres, I had 36 different sponsors that I was responsible for. Not just find them and sell them but service them once they came aboard. Trust me, that kept me hopping!

Developing the Mindset of "Going the Extra Mile"

But sponsorship execution is only one part of sponsorship activation.

In fact, it's actually the easier part of the equation because everything's written down. You agreed to do "x," so do it. But what about looking out for the undocumented interests of your sponsors?

Keep in mind the chief reason your sponsor opts to sign aboard with you isn't because they like you or like your event/publication.

It's because they're looking for new business, new sales. And that said, all the program ads and attendee badges in the world aren't going to help your renewal process if your sponsor can't show a return on their investment.

Keep in mind that if this doesn't work for your sponsor, if it fails to register at their cash register, no matter how diligent you are in executing the terms of your agreement, they're not coming back. Which means you'll be back at square one. And it's true what they say, it's seven to ten times harder to find a new sponsor than it is to keep an existing sponsor.

So keep your finger on their pulse. Check in frequently with them and see how they're doing. What are they looking for and what do they need? Many times you'll discover you can be of help to them in opening up doors and new avenues for them, well apart from what's in your contract, if only you ask.

I'll give you an example of one such case. I ran into one of our Sports Forum sponsors at another industry conference and we got to talking about their business. Eventually, it came out that they'd been trying to get a major piece of business with an NFL team but they didn't feel they were getting much traction.

I happened to know the vice president they were dealing with and took it upon myself to give my VP friend a call. On that call my friend told me that indeed he was about to pull the trigger on a deal that had possible league-wide repercussions, but he was leaning on going with one of my sponsor's competitors. I asked him if he had considered my sponsor? He responded that he had but that my sponsor was asking for more money than his other guys and that his other guys had offered to do a couple of other things for his team in addition.

I asked my friend that if I could get my sponsor to not only match the other guy's offer, but maybe do just a little bit better, would he consider giving the business to my sponsor?

He said he would. So I hung up, called my sponsor and dictated to him what he needed to do to get the business. As a result, he got himself the deal. And oh, by the way, we got ourselves a five year renewal on our sponsorship!

Now we certainly didn't have to do that. It wasn't in our contract. But I think it's one of the reasons why our sponsors tend to come back year after year.

So don't limit yourself to just what's in the contract. Keep in tune with their business and keep in touch with your sponsor. You never know when you'll be able to add that little extra that will make all the difference.

And one more thought on helping your sponsors to activate their sponsorship with you. Make sure they're using all the benefits they've bought from you in your package. Admittedly that may sound strange. After all, as long as you give it to them, who cares what they do with it, right?

Well, not always. Sponsorship benefits that don't get used are basically worthless. And they won't count as brownie points in their renewal consideration with you. For instance, back in my Padres days, one of our standard sponsor benefits would invariably be a block of tickets we'd give our sponsor to their night. For example, if it were a major promotional night, such as cap night, the sponsor would receive a block of 250 to 500 tickets to the game as part of their package. They could in turn use these tickets to send out to their branches to use in entertaining managers, employees, or VIP customers.

I noticed with one of my sponsors that the seats we'd pulled for their company hadn't been used on their night. I was curious as to what happened, and so I called and asked them about it.

My contact there sheepishly replied she'd been too slammed with other responsibilities to get the tickets out into their stores in time for them to be used. As a result, they wound up sitting there in her desk drawer.

What a waste, and, for many reasons, her loss was our loss.

But rather than say, "Oh well"—after all, we'd certainly sent her their tickets on time—I asked her if maybe next time we could help? I told her that if she'd simply have her assistant send me over a roster of their stores and how many tickets each was to get and we'd take care of getting them distributed to the organizations ourselves.

She sent the list and the next year we drop-shipped their tickets as she directed, thereby freeing her up to worry about other things. And, in those cases where the stores were relatively close to our stadium, I had an intern hand-deliver their packet of tickets to the store manager complete with a smile and one of our Padres baseball caps.

Believe me, the word got back to my sponsor—the store managers loved the personal touch. She looked like a star, and I got no argument when I increased their sponsorship fee in the next contract.

So keep this in mind where it comes to sponsorship – activation is everything. If you can't help to make it work for them, they won't come back. And that won't work for you.

Chapter Seventeen

"Let's Do It Again!"

It's ALL About the Renewals

We certainly touched on this in the last chapter, but it certainly bears repeating. Anything worth having is worth keeping—and that goes doubly with your sponsors.

Treated right, your sponsors will not only continue to supply you with much-needed capital, but they'll also become some of the greatest ambassadors for your publication, group or association out there in the market. And, why not, after all, your success means their success! Maybe in the start there was some strong residual value to their being affiliated with you. But as you continue to grow and prosper, you'll see that, over time, there's marked value for them being affiliated with you!

Final Thoughts About "Walking your Talk"

Be loyal to your sponsors, believe me, it gets noticed. Even when you don't think they're paying attention, they are.

If your sponsor is Toyota for example, don't be driving around in a Ford. If your event is affiliated with Coca-Cola, don't have Pepsi products in the speaker ready room. Use your head, little things make a big difference.

For example, we've long been affiliated with Budweiser. They've been a "proud sponsor of the National Sports Forum" for seven years now, and I hope they'll stay with us for another seven and then some.

That's why for us, you won't find any other beer at a Sports Forum event. Often times we'll have representatives from some of the other big beer sponsors, Coors, Miller Lite and so forth attending the Sports Forum. But if they want a beer, they're welcome to it, but it's going to be a Bud. We don't serve anything else. In fact, it's stipulated as such in our hotel contracts. For those guys, we keep the bar stocked with soda. They're welcome to drink those.

And from time to time we may put on other smaller conferences. We just put on, for instance, a small 50-person conference called The National Sports Forum Executive Retreat. Budweiser wasn't a sponsor of that event, but it was still the only beer we allowed served at the retreat. We are just as dedicated to all of our sponsors.

Now I don't know if Budweiser has noticed our loyalty or not, the company has never actually commented on it. But all too often other sponsors are focused on making sure you walk your talk. For instance, in our bi-annual NSF Corporate & Industry Survey a couple years ago, our interviewer got into an interesting conversation with one of the biggest office supply companies in America today. This company annually spends millions of dollars sponsoring different sports teams throughout the country, including several million dollars sponsoring one of the Big Four leagues.

At the end of the interview, our researcher asked the company exec the same question we conclude all of our interviews with, "What's the one thing you would want sports teams in general and sports sponsorship salespeople specifically to know when it comes to doing business with you?"

Without any hesitation the office supply marketing head replied, "If you take my money, you need to do business with me."

A bit confused, our interviewer asked the executive to kindly explain. And boy did she ever! She went on to say that despite all the millions of dollars that her organization spent on sponsoring this league, they couldn't begin to express the level of their disappointment over the fact that only three of the teams in the entire league had accounts with their company. Only three! The rest, she figured, apparently bought their office supplies from the competition.

Now that might seem like a little thing to you—but not to your sponsors. To your sponsors, little things mean everything.

Which is why it's so important you build sponsor loyalty into the fabric of the way you do business. Keep your sponsors forefront in mind—not only with your members and attendees, but introduce them and encourage interaction by and between all of your different sponsors. Many times one of the biggest sponsor benefits they will receive is the ability to do business with each other and help each other out.

Remember, if something is worth having, it's worth keeping. And keeping your sponsors active and engaged throughout the year can make a dramatic difference in keeping them happy and you very profitable!

Here's wishing you great success as you set out on this truly lucrative course of business. It's a lot of fun and in most cases sponsorship doesn't really cost you much more than what you're paying now to put on your event. But the difference, well, that can make all the difference in the world!

READY...AIM ... FIRE!

Go get 'em!

CPSIA information can be obtained at www.ICGtesting.com
Printed in the USA
BVOW051614180911

271497BV00007B/1/P